DEFEATING BREAST CANCER

DEFEATING BREAST CANCER

*A Physician's Story of
Healing, Martial Arts and Life*

Stacey Keen, M.D.

iUniverse, Inc.
New York Lincoln Shanghai

DEFEATING BREAST CANCER
*A Physician's Story of
Healing, Martial Arts and Life*

All Rights Reserved © 2004 by Stacey Keen, M.D.

No part of this book may be reproduced or transmitted in any form or by any means, graphic, electronic, or mechanical, including photocopying, recording, taping, or by any information storage retrieval system, without the written permission of the publisher.

iUniverse, Inc.

For information address:
iUniverse, Inc.
2021 Pine Lake Road, Suite 100
Lincoln, NE 68512
www.iuniverse.com

In telling the story of her journey through breast cancer, Dr. Keen relays not only her mental and emotional journey, but also her experience with complementary medicine, along with her traditional course of treatment through surgery, followed by chemotherapy and radiation therapy. Dr. Keen's goal in telling her story of breast cancer survival is to bring encouragement and hope to the lives of others struggling with breast cancer specifically, and life threatening illnesses in general. Dr. Keen's individual decision to embrace or reject any treatment alternative is not intended to be either an endorsement or rejection of a particular course of treatment for others, nor is any opinion expressed intended as medical advice to others. As is always the case, when under the care of a treating physician, it is important to confer with your physician before embarking on an alternative course of treatment.

ISBN: 0-595-33603-5

Printed in the United States of America

Dedicated to the memory of Sabra Jones, M.D., who inspired me to climb the highest peaks.

Contents

Introduction xi
Chapter 1 A Break from the Routine…Mammogram 1
Chapter 2 Surgery: Sword at the Heart 17
Chapter 3 The Results 23
Chapter 4 Planning the Course 28
Chapter 5 Getting Pumped 32
Chapter 6 Initiation 39
Chapter 7 Look Ma No Hair 45
Chapter 8 Round Two 49
Chapter 9 Mama's Here for You 53
Chapter 10 Happy New Year 56
Chapter 11 Halftime 59
Chapter 12 Here's Looking at Yew 67
Chapter 13 From Winter to Spring 72
Chapter 14 Celebration 76
Chapter 15 On Hiatus 79
Chapter 16 Catching Some Rays 83
Chapter 17 Back on the Road Again 87
Epilogue 95

Glossary.. 97
References... 103

Acknowledgements

Defeating Breast Cancer is a tribute to all of you whose support boosted me through one of life's challenging times. Your acts of kindness and love, too numerous to cite in these pages, will always be remembered.

Since writing this book, I have met others instrumental in getting it published. In particular, I would like to thank Cheryl Burk Leonardi, M.D. for introducing me to Diane Anselmo, who helped guide me toward my chosen dream. Also, I am grateful for the friendship and encouragement of Tina Beerman, traveling with me along the path of survivorship, patient care, enlightenment, and the synergy of Eastern and Western medicine.

Introduction

As a radiologist specializing in breast imaging, I have lectured to women's groups and talked on the radio. The topic has been "Screening Saves Lives," the importance of mammographic screening in reducing mortality from breast cancer.

Breast cancer is a subject near and dear to my heart—literally, as I had a mammographically detected malignancy deep in the 6 o'clock position of my left breast, right over my heart. In the hope that my journey through cancer and its therapy could help others facing the disease, I've recorded the events and thoughts of that life-changing experience.

I was fortunate to have had excellent treatment and support and to have weathered the therapy smoothly. That's not to say it is always easy. Since there have been so many frightful accounts of chemotherapy and cancer treatments, I wanted to relay an example of it going well, with life continuing on around it. My goal is to replace fear of the unknown with knowledge and hope for those facing similar situations.

While I describe successful breast cancer therapy, not all of those with the disease will have this outcome. It is estimated that 40,000 of my sisters in the struggle will succumb to breast cancer in 2004.[1] Whatever the result, my advice is to eke the most out of every moment of life, to deal with this fierce enemy head on, with courage, and to keep fighting, undaunted. No matter what.

Having studied martial arts for fourteen years, I've found that it has shaped my way of thinking, my attitude toward challenging situations. While not everyone out there is a student of the martial arts, it can serve as a useful metaphor for dealing with adversity.

With due respect to patient confidentiality, the cases I describe do not refer to actual individuals but are composites of my experiences over the years.

One caveat: my approach to the subject of breast cancer is lighter than that of many others. This reflects my worldview. By nature, I'm a laugher. The more serious a situation becomes, the greater my urge for levity. I confess to occasional fits of uncontrollable hysterical laughter at such inopportune times as graduations and religious services. If humor promotes healing,[2,3] let's keep rolling in the aisles.

Humor, positive attitude, and the best of Eastern and Western philosophy and medicine: I enlisted them all to maximize my chances of survival and to grow through this experience. Those who seek a somber tome about breast cancer should look elsewhere. Those who stay with me through these pages will glimpse a way of coping with cancer that I hope can brighten their lives.

References:

1. Jemal A, Tiwari RC, Murray T, et al. Cancer Statistics, 2004. CA Cancer J Clin 2004;54:8-29.

2. Seaward BL. Humor's healing potential. Health Prog 1992;73:66-70.

3. Erdman L. Laughter therapy for patients with cancer. Oncol Nurs Forum 1991;18:1359-1363.

1

A Break from the Routine...Mammogram

Shi-kin hara-mitsu dai-ko-myo: "Every encounter could represent the one potential key to...enlightenment."
Sen-sei ni-rei: "Bow to salute the teacher."
O-ne-gai-shi-mas: "Please assist me."[1]
So begins each class in Bujinkan Ninpo Taijutsu, the 900-year-old art of Japanese warriors. The art grew out of individuals protecting their families in feudal Japan. It began as men and women trained, using the tools around them, to fight for their way of life.

My children and I have been training in this Japanese martial art for 14 years. We began when Rachel was 8 and Michael was 5. People come to study Taijutsu from a variety of backgrounds. Some, formerly or currently in the military, see it as a continuation of their martial training. Others experience it as an epiphany; kids may want to learn to protect themselves from bullies; women may seek instruction in self-defense. Michael started training because my friend Sandie's son had been taking karate for a couple of years and liked it. For Rachel, it was a combination of the gymnastics and ballet that she had done in the past. I didn't intend to do karate at all. I was considering taking tap dancing classes with one of my friends. I thought I was too old to be starting something like karate, but then came the children's introductory lessons and I met my sensei, Mrs. Elrod. She invited me to try introductory lessons as well. When I professed to be too old, Mrs. Elrod hastened to introduce me to Mr. Ford, then 79 years old and nearly at black belt level.

Thus I began as an unlikely warrior, a mother sharing an activity with her two children. As our knowledge of katas and techniques grew over the years, so did our strength, stamina, perseverance, and fighting attitude. I'd advise anybody who intends to get breast cancer to train in martial arts beforehand. Enduring against all odds. The symbol "Nin" 忍 signifies patience, perseverance: even when a sword is at your heart you will prevail.

Each ninjutsu class commences with the above directives to focus our minds and bodies on the tasks before us. In every moment there is the potential for enlightenment, if only we're aware enough to perceive it. Teacher, please teach me.

> *There are so many teachers around us. I've learned so much from my children, my patients, as well as my family, friends, and colleagues.*

There were at least 29 bulldogs under the tent on Cross Campus that bright, warm October Saturday. It was Parents' weekend at Yale and kick-off of the tercentennial celebration. The Bulldog Club of Connecticut had arranged this gathering of Yale's mascots. The original plan was to get them into a formation of the letter Y, but the logistics of aligning the bow-legged stout pooches were too daunting. Rachel and I contented ourselves petting them and doling out tummy rubs. We followed a procession to nearby Beinecke Plaza for the cake presentation. It was the most enormous cake we'd ever seen, designed in replica of the Old Campus, the freshman quadrangle with Yale's oldest buildings. With all the people there I was glad to even get a slice, although I had been hoping for a piece of Vanderbilt, my old dorm.

In the early afternoon Rachel and I took a shuttle bus over to the Yale Bowl for the game against Penn. First, we dropped by the tailgate parties. There were elaborate tents from the frats and residential colleges, as well as the usual picnicking alums and students. The air was filled with aromas of barbecue and beer. I had a freshly grilled hamburger with everything on it, and Rachel ate a similarly equipped veggie burger. We chatted with her friends, some with their parents along. Rachel regaled me with stories of college life. We purchased my ticket and went into the Bowl for the game, just in time to see the Yale Precision Marching Band scramble onto the field, running chaotically into formation. Parents who were old band members were encouraged to join them during Parents' weekend. I stayed in my seat, choosing not to mortify Rachel by charging onto the field clutching my tambourine. Rachel explained the plays and pointed out her friends on the football team. Jay ran some impressive yardage, but we were behind at halftime when we left following the band show.

The Payne Whitney gym is an enormous Gothic structure. Many stories high, it's equipped with just about everything a university needs: tracks, swimming pools, fencing, volleyball, and who knows what else to fill all those floors. The weight room is spacious, bright, filled with blue and white machines. It wasn't at all crowded late on a football Saturday afternoon. Most of the machines were familiar from our neighborhood gym at home, but there were a few Rachel had to show me how to set.

Catey and Karen, two of Rachel's roommates from the previous year, joined us for dinner, along with Karen's parents. We ate Ethiopian food with flatbread and no silverware. It's always exciting to hear about classes, the many campus events and the sports teams. Yale had pulled ahead in the second half of the football game to beat Penn 27 to 24.

Rachel and Karen had both applied to the Birthright program, to visit Israel during winter break. Karen's parents were reluctant to let her go in light of the risks, but Rachel and I were sure that the students would be kept in safe locations.

We couldn't linger at dinner, as Rachel had to join the orchestra in Woolsey Hall, Yale's concert hall, by 7:30 p.m. The concert was a lively one, featuring the glee club, Yale Symphony, and the jazz band. Rachel had some beautiful flute parts. I met several of her orchestra buddies and got to chat with the conductor in the reception following the concert.

The weekend went all too quickly. I read on the Amtrak ride back to Maryland and called my son Michael on my cell phone to find out about his PSAT (the reason he and his Dad, my husband AJ, hadn't accompanied me to New Haven). This high school junior year was what Michael and I termed the Year Of The Evaluation. It seemed that every time he turned around there was another standardized test or some sort of musical competition. He responded that the PSAT had gone pretty well. One test down!

The next day, Monday, October 23, 2000 started out innocently as an ordinary day, but turned out to be one that changed the course of my life. I'm a radiologist and was working part-time, with Mondays and Tuesdays off. AJ and I went out to breakfast at one of our favorite bagel places. There I told him about my weekend with Rachel in New Haven, and he filled me in on his time with Michael at home.

At 9 am, I had my routine annual appointment with Barbara Phillips-Seitz, my colleague and gynecologist. No complaints, but I was wondering what to expect during this perimenopausal time, as I was 46. I also pointed out a tender spot in the 6 o'clock position of my left breast that had been there at least a year. I noticed a nodular area there on breast self-exam, but it would become less prominent and less sore after I'd get my period, so I figured it was a cyst. Barbara did feel something on her examination, although it was deep, up against the rib. She noted the area of soreness on my mammogram request. I had already scheduled my mammo appointment for later that day to get all of my appointments over with.

I arrived at my office at 1:30 to fill out the insurance forms and medical questionnaires prior to my 1:45 appointment. My dear friend and colleague Jessie Stahl was working at our office that day.

We chatted just a short while before Susan Birbiglia, the mammography technologist, told me she was ready to do my exam. Susan, like me, was originally from New York, but she was a Mets fan and I'm a Yankees fan. I decided not to mention that the Yanks were up on the Mets two games to none in the first subway series in forty-four years until AFTER she'd done the mammogram compression.

I dressed in one of those medical gowns, peach-colored, with armhole openings halfway down your sides.

"Lovely, isn't it?" I commented to Susan, as we entered the mammo room. This is where I'd go and talk to patients about their results, and now I was on the receiving end of the vise.

I let Susan do all the positioning. As anxious as I was to help, I knew she'd be much better off just doing her usual routine without my input. I mentioned the area in the back of my lower left breast that I noticed.

Mammograms aren't pleasant, but they're over with quickly. The compression of the machine lasts less than half a minute for each of the 4 views, so how bad could it be? As soon as that last shot was completed, I had to mention how well those Yankees were doing.

When we were done, Susan ran the films in the darkroom. I walked out to the processor to pick them up. That's one advantage of being a radiologist: you get your results immediately, without having to wait days for an official report. Our CT tech, Sara Winter, was between patients, so she waited with me.

I put up the films on the nearby viewbox, lining them up as I always do, right and left mediolateral oblique(side to side) and craniocaudad (up and down) views side by side. I went through my usual pattern of looking at mammograms, systematically checking, starting with the right oblique mediolateral view, from superior to inferior (top to bottom) and posterior to anterior (back to front) in the breast, scanning the dense stroma (glandular tissue) and surrounding fatty tissue. Then onto the left oblique mediolateral, same thing, looking for symmetry, scanning fibroglandular and fatty tissue.

There was a cluster of microcalcifications (tiny calcium deposits) in the posterior inferior left breast, near the inframammary fold (the lowest breast tissue), in an area so far back that it was difficult to include entirely on the film. That Susan is a good tech. The inframammary fold region is not always included on mammograms, even though it should be. Microcalcifications, with some associated increased density. Could it be an artifact? Let's see where they are on the craniocaudad view. Not there, too far back and not included on that view.

"I guess we need some magnified views," I told Susan and Sara. I looked at my watch. It was getting towards 2 o'clock and Michael was due home from school at 2:45.

"Why don't I do the mags tomorrow?" I suggested. By this time, though, Jessie was looking at the films with us.

"You're not leaving until the mags are done," Jessie pronounced. I felt bad about disrupting Susan's schedule. After all, I was in just for a 15-minute screening slot, and here I was taking up more time. They'd have none of my excuses.

Susan took me right back into the mammo suite to contort me in an attempt to get views farther back in my left breast than I ever thought possible: mags in the MLO and CC views and a 90 degree mediolateral view.

This time, waiting for the films to emerge from the processor, there was grim silence. I took each film from the slot in the processor and placed them on the viewbox.

"That looks like DCIS [ductal carcinoma in situ]," I commented. Those were not indeterminate microcalcifications, they were malignant ones.

I took my mammogram over to Jessie, sitting at the mammo viewer. She eyed my films carefully with a magnifying glass.

"Stace, I want you to see a surgeon right away. Call Barbara now for a referral. See who she recommends."

"I know the names of the two best breast surgeons in Baltimore," I said. "I don't want to see anyone locally in town because I've worked with most of them, and they know me." I preferred to be anonymous when receiving health care. Even when Rachel and Michael were born, I made sure to go to a hospital not affiliated with my residency program.

I dressed quickly; it was 2:35 and I wanted to get home to Michael.

"Promise me you'll call Barbara and a surgeon as soon as you get home," said Jessie, giving me a hug.

"I will."

As I got into the car, I called AJ at his lab from my cell phone.

"I can't talk long, because I'm driving home now to Michael," I began, "but I have to tell you. My mammogram looks really suspicious. I've got to have a biopsy."

He'd been through this with his mom four years before. She'd had a needle localization and biopsy for a tiny noninvasive cancer, DCIS. Easy surgery. She went out shopping afterwards.

"It's a group of calcifications, way in the back of my left breast. They look like DCIS."

AJ's voice sounded grave: "What do you need to do next?"

"I'm going to call my gynecologist Barbara for a surgery referral. I'm also thinking of showing my films to Judy to see what she recommends." Dr. Judy

Destouet is head of mammography in my radiology group of about 90, renowned nationally in the field. I was fortunate to have the opportunity to work with her, reading mammograms and doing biopsies at our main mammography facility.

"Do you need me to come home?" he asked.

"No, I'm okay," I replied.

Michael was just getting home from marching band rehearsal when I arrived. He was one of the two drum majors.

"Hi Mike. How was rehearsal?"

"It went okay. We ran through the half-time show a few times."

"You've got so many talented musicians in your group. Anything interesting happen in your classes?"

"Not much," he replied. High school boys don't go in for detail.

"I just had my mammogram, and it was abnormal, with a group of suspicious looking calcifications, so I'm going to need a biopsy," I told him. I don't believe in hiding things from my children. They'd find out anyway, and it's best to hear it from me, so I could explain the medical aspects accurately.

"I'm going to call my doctor for a referral to a surgeon." I was pretty matter of fact about the whole thing. After all, I faced this sort of thing daily at my work, and I didn't want to seem too alarmed about the matter. The only thing was it was *my* body that needed the biopsy.

I love Michael's attitude, a refreshing, hilarious irreverence. After a few minutes he said:

"Now you can go into the Survivor Tent at the Race for the Cure and get your own doughnut." I had run the race three weeks previously with my friend Bonnie, and had spoken enviously of the doughnut she got.

"Not only that," I added, "at the next Race for the Cure, I'll get to wear my own pink runner's number and have my name announced as I run through the finish line!"

I did as Jessie recommended and called Barbara right away. I asked which of the two breast surgeons in the city she'd recommend. She said she'd had patients go to both and they were very pleased. I thought I'd be more comfortable seeing the female surgeon, Dr. Lauren Schnaper.

It was a little hard to concentrate on making dinner, but I had to get Michael to his piano lesson on time. The way I cooked it, pasta wasn't a particularly demanding dish. But I felt restless. I decided to call Judy at home.

"Judy, this is Stacey Keen. I'm calling because I had an abnormal mammogram, and I'd like you to review it."

"Stacey, I'd be happy to."

"It's a new cluster of microcalcifications that look like DCIS," I described.

"I'll be at the mammo center tomorrow," Judy continued. "Can you be there by 8:30?"

"I've got a dental appointment at 9, but I can be there between 10 and 10:30."

"That will be fine. Come whenever you can."

"Thank you so much, I really appreciate it."

At times like this, the children and I have a tradition of baking. Michael and I were really in the mood for some M&M cookies. The only problem: no M&M's! After dinner, AJ and I headed over to the store for the chocolate. Chocolate really does make things better. In the checkout line, AJ happened to spot *Baltimore* magazine, featuring its annual issue on the best doctors in the area. We scanned it for breast surgeons. There she was, Dr. Schnaper. I copied her office address and telephone number from the magazine. All thanks to chocolate for locating my breast surgeon!

The distraction of baking couldn't keep the mammogram off my mind. I called my friend Bonnie, who had been through breast cancer surgery one year previously. When I told her, she said it just didn't seem right that her doctor should be getting this. It does overturn a sort of natural order of things, doesn't it?

Next I called Bob Sheff, former chief of radiology and now head of my medical group, to see how I could see a surgeon not enrolled in our medical roster.

"Hello Bob, this is Stacey Keen."

"Hi! How's it going?"

"Things could be better. I had a mammogram today, and there's a suspicious cluster of microcalcifications that really look like DCIS."

"Stace, I'm so sorry to hear that. Is there anything I can do for you?"

"Well, yes, as a matter of fact. I was thinking of seeing the breast surgeon Dr. Schnaper downtown. I feel a little weird seeing someone around here whom I've worked with. How do I arrange to go out of plan?"

"Not a problem. I'll call the chief of referrals tomorrow and take care of it. Who's your primary care?"

"Dr. Bensinger."

"How are you doing?"

"Okay, considering. I called Dr. Destouet, and she's going to take a look at my mammogram tomorrow morning. I just want to get this taken care of as soon as possible. This is such a major inconvenience."

"That's one way of looking at it. Try to get some sleep tonight, though. Call me tomorrow after you speak to Dr. Destouet, and I'll arrange the referral."

"Thanks."

Getting some sleep was next to impossible. There was just no way I could rest until I knew the diagnosis for sure. My thoughts raced all night: it was kind of deep in the breast to do a stereotactic core biopsy. Maybe Judy will think I should go straight to preoperative needle localization and excisional biopsy. There was no way those calcifications were benign. Probably just DCIS, requiring lumpectomy and radiation therapy. My mother-in-law went through that. Took it like a champ. The radiation was a little tiring and the spot a little itchy, but that was it. Lumpectomy and radiation. That's not too bad. But how soon can I get that done? The suspense is killing me. I just want to get this taken care of. How much time would I need off from work?

The next morning after my dental appointment, I hightailed it around the Beltway to Dr. Destouet's office. I walked in, mammo films in hand.

"Hi! Are you busy right now?" I asked hesitantly.

"No, come on in. Let me take a look at it," said Judy.

"Thank you so much. I think it looks like DCIS."

I sat looking the other way as Judy pored over my films at a viewbox.

"You need a biopsy. Can you feel anything there?" she asked.

"Well, I've noticed a sore spot and a small knot that comes and goes with my cycle."

"I think we should do an ultrasound, to see if it shows up. It would be easier to biopsy under ultrasound if we could see it, because it's so far back to stereo." Within five minutes I was lying on the ultrasound table, slathered in gel, peering at the small screen with Judy and the technologist, Wanda. We could see a mass associated with the calcifications. Judy put the calipers on it: 1.5 x 1.4x 1.0 cm…that was out of the minimal cancer range. It was way back in the 6 o'clock position of the breast and tender when she scanned it.

"We'll see if Rosy Singh can do the ultrasound-guided biopsy tomorrow," said Judy.

Wanda looked at the schedule and said "There's an opening 8:30 tomorrow morning."

"I'll take it!" I said. "Now I just have to call Vicki to get off the work schedule for tomorrow."

"I'm sure that won't be a problem," said Judy.

"I was thinking of seeing Dr. Schnaper," I said. "Do you know her?"

"Oh yes, I've worked with her quite a bit. Let me give her office a call and see how soon she can get you in. She likes to have the core biopsy results when she sees her patients, though."

When I was dressed and sitting in Judy's office she made the call. Dr. Schnaper usually sees new patients on Tuesdays. Was there any way she could get me in sooner? That was a week from now. I couldn't wait a whole week. Yes, there was an opening this Friday. Eight-thirty a.m. The core biopsy results should be ready by then. I needed to bring my mammogram and ultrasound films and the pathology report from the core biopsy.

At home I went back to the telephone. The first call was to AJ, letting him know the schedule of events. Then I called Vicki, in charge of the group's schedule. I told her the situation, and that I needed to be off the rest of the week. She was very sympathetic, assuring me that it would be no problem and wishing me luck.

The next call was to my friend the pathologist. We used to run a mammography/pathology correlation conference together. I told him that I was scheduled for a core biopsy of a suspicious looking lesion the next day. Would he be able to read out the results right away before my surgeon's appointment Friday? Absolutely; he would arrange it. I told him I'd hand-deliver my specimen to the lab.

I spoke to Bob for the referral to Dr. Schnaper. After that I telephoned my sister, Leslie. I didn't want to worry Mom, but I thought someone in the family needed to know what was up. Jessie called back to make sure I'd contacted a surgeon. So much to think about-my head was spinning. I decided to work out at the gym.

Another fitful night's sleep. After Michael left for school, AJ and I headed for the mammography center. I signed in. We sat in the waiting room. Strange to be sitting here on the other side as a patient. Dr. Singh, looking very somber, came out to greet me. I introduced her to AJ and then followed her back. No need for AJ to come with me-he'd just get in the way, and you never know when those husbands are going to pass out on you.

I did not envy Rosy her position: core biopsy on a colleague's suspicious looking lesion, deep in the breast near the chest wall. No, that would be a stressful position to be in, although mine was no walk in the park either.

Rosy and Wanda left the ultrasound room so I could change into the patient gown, opening in the front. Suitably attired, I sat up on the ultrasound table and waited for them to return, waited alone with my thoughts. At this point, they weren't thoughts, so much as prayers. I was praying as hard as I ever remember praying in my life not just for me and a benign result, but for God to guide Rosy's hands through the procedure.

Wanda returned first and gave me the consent form to read and sign. How many times I've reviewed that form with my patients! It seemed odd to be signing my name on the line for the patient rather than the physician.

Wanda positioned me on the ultrasound table: turned a little to the right, with my left arm resting on the pillow above my head. Rosy came in and scanned me first, to see where the lesion was and what approach to take. Since it was a lesion in the left breast, she decided to stand by my left side, which entailed moving the ultrasound table away from the wall a bit. I watched the ultrasound screen as she scanned. It was not a pretty looking mass and to my trained eye looked suspicious for malignancy.

Rosy donned her sterile gloves. Wanda was an excellent, experienced technologist, handing Rosy needles, syringes, and anesthetic without Rosy having to say a word. They worked together as one.

After scrubbing my skin with betadine to create a sterile field, Rosy placed a sterile drape with a hole in the center (I've always loved the fancy medical term for that, a fenestrated drape) over my left breast. With Wanda's assistance, she placed a sterile cover resembling an elephant condom (or what I'd imagine an elephant condom would look like, as I've never really seen one), over the ultrasound probe (transducer).

After placing sterile ultrasound gel on my skin, Rosy began to scan my lower left breast. I thought watching the ultrasound screen would be far more entertaining than watching Rosy actually place a 14 gauge needle into my flesh, so that's where I kept my gaze.

"First I'm going to give you the local," Rosy warned, "you'll feel a stick and a stinging." She was right.

I continued watching the screen as she made a teeny incision in my skin with a scalpel and placed the biopsy needle adjacent to the mass.

"Okay, here it goes, I'm going to take the first sample: one, two, three!" The needle traversed the middle of the mass. That wasn't too bad, just a brief stinging sensation. Rosy did a good job: through the center of the lesion, not into my underlying heart or lung!

I typically take about five samples through a mass unless I'm not getting adequate tissue samples, in which case I'll elect to do more. After five samples Rosy said:

"I'd like to get two more samples, to be sure we have enough tissue, if that's all right with you."

"Of course," I said, as if I really had a choice. If we were going to all this trouble, I wanted the specimen to be adequate.

All the samples were placed in a jar of formalin preservative. Rosy applied pressure to the biopsy site for ten minutes to stop the bleeding and limit hematoma formation. She then placed two thin Steri-Strips directly over the skin nick and a pressure bandage dressing over the breast.

"Sleep in a sports bra tonight. If you notice some soreness in the area when the anesthesia wears off, in three to four hours, you can take Tylenol. Try to keep ice on it today."

"When can I exercise?" I was hoping life would be back to normal as soon as possible.

"You can do lower body tomorrow, but I'd give it an extra day or two before you do lifting with your arms," Rosy replied. She handed me a sheet of instructions with her beeper number. "Call me if you need anything."

"Thank you so much for getting me on the schedule today," I told her. I got dressed and left the room carrying my mammograms, ultrasound films, and a specimen bag containing the little jar of tissue samples.

AJ was there in the waiting room.

"Did you finish the crossword puzzle?" I asked.

"Never mind that," he said. "How did it go? Did Rosy use a harpoon?"

"It wasn't too bad," I reassured him. "Now we have to go straight to the lab, so I can deliver this specimen."

When we arrived in the Pathology department, I handed off my specimen to Pam, the secretary I'd worked with for years. She was the one who sent me path reports every month for the mammography/pathology correlation I did on all the breast biopsies. Now it was my own specimen under the microscope.

Pam was quite concerned for me, hoping that my result would be a good one. The specimen would be processed immediately and the results available the next morning. The doctor would give me a call. I explained that my appointment with the surgeon Dr. Schnaper was Friday, and I needed the path report faxed to her by then.

"Not a problem," assured Pam, "I'll take care of it."

AJ dropped me off at home, walked our dog Meg and left for work. I sat down on the couch trying to read and get my mind off of the immediate situation. Meg lay down at my feet, and one of my cats, Micetro, jumped into my lap and started purring. Somehow animals seem to sense when you need comforting. Jessie's daughter Jennifer has a theory that pets are angels who watch over you. At times like this I could easily believe it.

I was glad to have the rest of the day off, because I did not feel focused enough to work. Somehow, it would have been hard to concentrate on the health of others. The area of the biopsy was a little sore a couple of hours later, and I took two Tylenol, as Rosy had suggested.

Okay, so if it's DCIS, I'll get a lumpectomy and radiation therapy and that's it. No big deal. I hear you can still work during radiation, that you just feel a little tired towards the end.

To take my mind off of weightier matters, I uncharacteristically planted myself in front of the TV. At least the Yanks took game four of the World Series.

The next morning, AJ took me out to breakfast at a local muffin shop, a pleasant distraction from the impending phone call. I did the crossword, checked e-mail, petted the dog.

At 10:30 a.m. the phone rang. It was the pathologist. Pathologists are not usually the ones to give patients their results, but as a colleague I was an exception. He sounded grim:

"I've got bad news for you," he started, with difficulty. I thought I'd help him out a little bit.

"I know, it's DCIS, isn't it?"

"Yes, but there are also areas of infiltrating ductal carcinoma."

"Infiltrating also?" I echoed, to be sure I was hearing him correctly.

"Yes, there are several areas showing infiltrating ductal carcinoma."

"Would you be able to fax the report to Dr. Schnaper's office for my appointment tomorrow?"

"Certainly," he said.

"I really appreciate your calling." I told him.

"Not a problem. Good luck with everything," he said gravely.

Infiltrating ductal carcinoma. I can't believe it. I thought it was just going to be DCIS. This is worse than I thought. Crap. Infiltrating ductal carcinoma. This is the real thing: breast cancer. Why couldn't it just be DCIS? I have breast cancer. Man, I want that thing out of there as soon as possible. I hope Lauren can schedule the surgery soon.

I called AJ with my results. He took it in quietly. We were glad I had gotten in to see Dr. Schnaper so quickly.

I went to the mall to pick up some photos for Michael. As I walked past people, I'd think:

"Do you realize that I have breast cancer?"

I felt like a different person. I felt perfectly well. How could I have cancer? How am I going to feel after surgery and whatever follows? Why did I have to get this? It's just too coincidental. I'm the one who diagnoses other people with this disease by mammograms and biopsies. Now it's my turn. Jessie crystallized my thoughts. I remember one thing she said after her daughter Jennifer was diagnosed with brain cancer: she felt that all of her life had prepared her for that moment. God doesn't give you what you can't handle. I can handle this. This is a disease with which I'm all too familiar.

When Michael came home from school, I told him my path results, explaining that DCIS was non-invasive cancer within the ducts, but infiltrating ductal cancer had actually invaded the breast tissue which surrounded the ducts.

He took it all in and was silent for awhile. Then he said:

"You know, anybody who's anybody has had breast cancer."

"You're right! Everyone in Dad's family: Nana, Nana's sister, all of his cousins."

"Olivia Newton-John," Michael added.

"Nancy Reagan and Betty Ford had it too," I said.

As expressed by Lillie Shockney in her book, *Breast Cancer Survivor's Club: A Nurse's Experience,*

"To be a club member, you must have had breast cancer. It is obviously an elite club—not one for which you find membership forms in the back of a high-society magazine."[2]

Stace, welcome to the fold.

But Rachel, how and when to tell Rachel? A few minutes after Michael and I talked, Rachel called. She told me about her midterms (an A on her AIDS course exam). She was done with her major tests and assignments for the week. I decided to tell her about my week and my path results. Just last weekend we were together celebrating Yale's Tercentennial, and now this!

There was silence on the other end of the line as I told her about my screening mammogram, the ultrasound-guided biopsy, the pathology results. I reassured her that it had been caught early by mammography.

"Are you going to have surgery?" Rachel asked, her voice quivering.

"I have an appointment with Dr. Schnaper, one of the best breast surgeons in Baltimore tomorrow and then we'll schedule it. I'll probably just need lumpectomy and radiation, just like Nana had."

I could sense Rachel's world changing: concern for me and not being around while I was going through all this; implications for her own future risk of cancer.

"Rache, you'll just have to start getting mammograms at age 30."

Rachel got off the phone quickly after that. I could tell she needed time alone to think, to cry, to process all I'd told her.

Friday was another unusually warm October day. AJ and I drove almost an hour to Dr. Schnaper's office. I signed in, and the receptionist went over all of my insurance information. The office didn't usually take my insurance (I panicked briefly), but my referral to go out of plan had been received by fax the previous afternoon (thank you Bob!). My pathology report had been received as well.

I gave the receptionist my films for Dr. Schnaper to review. I then completed a questionnaire about my medical history. In a few minutes, a nurse escorted me back to the examination room. I dressed in one of those little patient gowns again. The nurse returned to get my vital signs.

"Dr. Schnaper doesn't usually see new cancer patients on Fridays," she began. "She likes to spend an hour and a half reviewing the mammograms and treatment options with them."

"I'm a radiologist, and I do a lot of mammography, so I'm very familiar with the choices," I explained.

Dr. Schnaper came in and introduced herself.

"Call me Lauren," she told me. I summarized the events of the past few days. She then performed a very thorough breast exam on me, also checking the lymph nodes in the axillae (underarms) and supraclavicular (above the collar bone) regions.

"How big was the lesion on ultrasound?"

"It was about 1.5cm," I replied.

Lauren commented that I felt cystic, which is what I had thought, so I didn't feel like I'd missed something big on self-examination.

"I don't feel any enlarged lymph nodes. That means only a 20% chance of positive nodes at biopsy." Fantastic!

She put my mammograms up on the viewbox.

"It's way in the back of the breast. It won't be an easy needle localization," I said.

"Dr. Alex Munitz is very good. Do you know him?" asked Lauren.

"He's in my group, but I haven't met him," I said; "Dr. Destouet has told me he's excellent."

"I usually take time to explain the treatment options to patients, but I guess I don't have to with you. Do you know about sentinel lymph node biopsy?"

"Yes," I answered. Sentinel lymph nodes refer to the first, lowest lymph nodes in the armpit that drain the tumor site. They're removed and the pathologist analyzes them under the microscope. If the sentinel nodes are free of tumor cells, the tumor is localized to the breast and has not spread to the lymph nodes.

"I use technetium sulfur colloid and blue dye to identify the sentinel nodes," she explained. State of the art, up on the latest and best techniques. I like Dr. Schnaper.

I didn't want to consider mastectomy unless there was no alternative (i.e., if there were margins positive for cancer, DCIS with extensive intraductal component, multicentric tumor, large lesion with poor cosmetic result). As far as surgery goes, I like the "less is more" approach. Why have something removed that doesn't need to be? Besides, there was literature indicating that breast conservation and radiation therapy resulted in recurrence and survival rates comparable to mastectomy. I even had a copy of the original *New England Journal of Medicine* article[3,4] in my files.

"I'll schedule you for a needle-guided excision with sentinel lymph node biopsy," said Lauren.

"How soon can you get me in?" I asked.

"I'll consult my schedule and check with the OR for times. You can get dressed and get your husband."

AJ came into the exam room, and I told him about my exam and discussion with Lauren. She returned a few minutes later:

"I checked with the OR. There's an opening Monday."

"That's great! I'll take it," I felt like I had the winning bid at an auction.

"The OR time is 12:30. We'll schedule your needle localization in Radiology for 7:30a.m. followed by the sentinel lymph node injection in Nuclear Medicine. You'll need a chest x-ray and some labwork done today."

"How long will it take to get the biopsy results?" I asked.

"It will take about three days. I'll be getting receptor and immunohistochemical stains on it. Make a follow-up appointment with me for next Friday to go over the results. Do you know of an oncologist to follow up with?"

"Oh yes, a colleague I've worked with for years, Jon Minford. Do you know him?"

"I've known him for at least 10 years, from University of Maryland."

"I'm so glad you were able to get me in this fast. We'll go right from here to the lab and Radiology," I said.

"Bring your films with you so Dr. Munitz can review them before the localization," Lauren advised. I could part with them for the weekend, but I was going to make sure I got them back right after my surgery.

AJ and I found our way to the lab and then the Radiology department. I'd never worked at this site. I was glad of that—I prefer to be anonymous when I'm on the receiving end of health care. I did know one of the technologists there, Sandy, who had been the supervisor at my office. She was a breast cancer survivor herself. Sandy did my chest x-ray, and I told her about my impending surgery.

She gave me a hug and heartfelt prayers, some of the best medicine I'd had all week.

When we arrived home, I called Dr. Minford's office for an appointment. I knew the number by heart, as I'd phoned in x-ray results so many times to my colleague over the years.

"This is Dr. Keen calling," I began as I usually did. This time, though, I added: "to make an appointment with Dr. Minford."

"When would you like to see him?" asked the receptionist.

"Is he available Tuesday, November 7?"

"Yes, there's an opening at 9 a.m."

"That's fine," I said.

"Your diagnosis?"

"Breast cancer."

References:

1. Hayes, SK. *Enlightened Self-Protection: The Kasumi-An Ninja Arts Tradition.* Nine Gates Press, 1992, p.21.

2. Shockney, L. *Breast Cancer Survivors' Club: A Nurse's Experience.* Real Health Books, 1999, p.8.

3. Fisher B, Bauer M, Margolese R, et al. Five-year results of a randomized clinical trial comparing total mastectomy and segmental mastectomy with or without radiation in the treatment of breast cancer. N Engl J Med 1985; 312:665-73.

4. Veronesi U, Cascinelli N, Mariani L, et al. Twenty-year follow-up of a randomized study comparing breast-conserving surgery with radical mastectomy for early breast cancer. N Engl J Med 2002;347:1227-1232.

2

Surgery: Sword at the Heart

Ukeme-rolling and falling. This includes soft and hard front and rear falls, forward and rear shoulder rolls, side rolls, dive rolls, and cartwheels, as well as jumping and ducking. Ukeme is crucial to learn in martial arts. Early in our training Mr. Ford taught us: "Think of the ground as your friend." Proper rolling and falling can prevent injury in many situations, not just a fight. At different times, both Rachel and Michael fell off bicycles and avoided injury by doing proper hard falls. I, myself, once slipped on ice while running, landing in a good hard fall and keeping my bones intact.

Learning ukeme has come easier to Rachel and Michael as kids than to me as an adult during the course of our training. Perhaps adults' greater distance from the ground in time and space makes them more frightened of it.

Dive rolls over obstacles were particularly challenging for me to learn. I've had swimming lessons and can do most of the strokes, but I've never learned how to dive, so the concept was not one familiar to my body. When we learned dive rolls at the red belt level, Rachel and Michael were highly amused by my initial attempts, or, I should say, ground flops. Persistence has paid off, and I can now clear at least a couple of bags with my forward dive roll.

There are a number of drills we do in class to practice ukeme. Standing in lines, we'll be pushed from behind and be required to absorb the energy of the attack, proceding into a forward roll, literally learning to roll with the punches. Similarly, when pushed from the front, we absorb the energy and go into a rear roll. When attacked with a sword, we are required to duck, jump, or roll out of the way, depending on the type of strike. We train our bodies to react without conscious thought.

I went to the dojo later on the same day I'd seen Dr. Schnaper. I thought it was time to inform my sensei, Mrs. Elrod, about what was happening with me and told her we needed to talk privately. As it was a warm, sunny afternoon, we walked outside. I told her my recent saga and about my upcoming surgery. I wasn't yet sure what treatment I would be getting after that.

Mrs. Elrod listened gravely; she'd lost her mother to the same disease a little over a year before.

"How are you doing?" she asked.

"I'm doing okay," I said to reassure myself as well as my teacher. "I'm not going to stop doing things I love, like training," I said.

"We'll adapt your training," she reassured me; "You'll do fine; you're a fighter."

Nin: even when a sword is at your heart you will prevail.

A few minutes after I arrived home, Jessie came by with a pot of chicken soup. She had seen a recent study claiming that it really did boost immunity.

That evening I called Debbie, my best friend since childhood who is like another sister to me. We talked our typical hour, although this time it revolved more around me than our usual give and take. Debbie's mother, a strong, vibrant woman, battled breast cancer successfully, only to succumb to complications of rheumatoid arthritis twenty-five years later. Debbie lived with her husband Peter and daughter Rebecca in New Hampshire, but said she would catch a flight down to see me whenever I needed her to.

I was determined to enjoy that pre-surgery weekend to the max. Saturday was a blustery, golden October day, with leaves falling in a steady flurry. We started out with my favorite: cinnamon scones at Barnes'n'Noble. AJ and I worked on the Sunday crossword puzzle and then went to the gym.

Debbie called back that evening. We decided it would be best if she arrived Monday night, after my surgery, and stayed through Wednesday. What a wonderful friend! With all the phone calls and activity, I joked to Michael that we hadn't had such a big social event since his Bar Mitzvah. I could sense that people were praying for me: I received a card from our office health assistant Angie, also signed by her priest.

One of the toughest phone calls to make was to my mother. How do you tell your mother that you, her baby, have breast cancer? Mothers love you so much, you hate to share such bad news. The last cancer in our immediate family was my father's Hodgkins lymphoma forty years ago, and he passed away from it. But mine was different. My breast cancer was mammographically detected, curable. I've seen hundreds of patients through this to the other side, and I see them years and years later, returning for their annual screening mammograms.

My mother took it all in. She thought it was no coincidence that I developed breast cancer. Mom is a strong believer in the body/mind connection, and felt that I, too caring a doctor, had taken on my patients' ailments. It wasn't any easier telling my brother Wayne. I'm the youngest. It just isn't right that I should come up with something like this. After all, he said, he was the one who used to smoke.

Bonnie came by with a care package Sunday evening. Having been through this surgery the year before, she was full of practical tips. In the care package were several buttondown shirts and sweaters, as well as stool softeners. For my surgery Monday, I decided to wear the lucky red denim shirt her brother had given her.

Sunday night I told Michael that Dad and I would be leaving early for my surgery on Monday morning. He'd have to wake up for school with the clock radio without my usual on site encouragement, but I would call to make sure he was awake. Sleeping was certainly a challenge that night, but I assured myself I'd get plenty of rest the next day under anesthesia.

We left the house a little after 6 a.m. to get to the medical center for check-in by 7. Not much traffic on the Beltway at that hour. Wouldn't it be great if we could just keep on driving north and go visit Rachel instead? I called Michael in the car from my cell phone. We'd be back home by about 6 p.m. I wished him a good day at school, and he wished me luck with the surgery.

The sun was just coming up when we arrived at the hospital. Dr. Schnaper's first patient, an elderly woman, was already in the waiting room with her family. AJ and I were somber as I signed the ream of forms. The one inquiring about a living will gave me the creeps. This was only outpatient surgery under local anesthesia with sedation. Why the heck were they asking me about a living will and what religion I was?

AJ and I then went to Radiology for my 7:30 a.m. needle localization appointment. I signed in at the receptionist's desk. There were already a couple of ultrasound and fluoroscopy patients waiting. One of the technologists called my name and I went in, leaving AJ in the company of a book.

I was shown to a small dressing room with a locker for my purse and instructed to open the curtain when I was finished changing into a patient gown. I was waiting for the technologist when Sandy came by.

"Patty will be the tech for your procedure. She's excellent." If Sandy said it, I knew it was true.

"I'd like you to have this angel to watch over you," she said. She handed me a pin, an angel with yellow hair and golden wings, holding a pink ribbon.

"She's beautiful!" I exclaimed, giving Sandy a big hug. I had just been properly initiated into the select group of breast cancer survivors.

Patty escorted me into the mammography suite for my needle localization. I've done hundreds of these in my career and knew exactly what to expect. Mine would be a particularly challenging one, due to the deep location of the lesion and the difficulty in seeing it well on two views. Since both Drs. Destouet and Schnaper had spoken highly of Dr. Munitz, I knew I would be in good hands.

Dr. Munitz came in to introduce himself. I signed the consent form. Patty then positioned me for the localization. Dr. Munitz thought an approach from beneath the breast, in the caudo-cranial position (compressed from above and below), would be best, as the lesion was in the 6 o'clock position and this would be the shortest distance to it. She took several exposures attempting to position the lesion in the field. No luck.

After consulting with Dr. Munitz, Patty turned the mammogram unit into the vertical medio-lateral position and took another shot. There it was. She showed the x-ray to Dr. Munitz, adjusted my position a little bit and took another exposure.

"Perfect! Stay just like that, now. Don't move," (as if I really had a choice clamped into that vise as I was).

Dr. Munitz returned. Through an opening in the compression paddle, he cleansed my skin with betadine. He then numbed my skin and placed the localization needle. Through its center, he threaded the hook wire. There, I thought, all done. Not so.

"I want to put in another wire to locate the edge of the lesion." If that would help Dr. Schnaper get the whole thing out with clear margins, then go ahead, I thought. After both wires were in place, Patty took another exposure. I looked down at the wires. I could see the deeper one moving with each heartbeat, as it was in the area right over my heart. Dr. Munitz viewed the last x-ray and said he would put in one more wire.

After the final wire was placed, Patty turned the machine into the perpendicular cranio-caudad projection, to adjust the depth. Once the three wires were in their final positions, Patty put a paper cup and a dressing over them, for stabilization until surgery.

AJ and an orderly whisked me by wheelchair to the Nuclear Medicine department for the next step, sentinel lymph node injection. There were several inpatients in the small Nuclear Medicine waiting room. AJ and I waited a few minutes until it was my turn.

I walked into the room with the radiation detecting gamma camera and was helped onto the table, guarding the three antennae-like wires in my breast. The technologist explained that she was going to make four small injections of the 99mTc Sulfur Colloid solution under my skin close to the site of the tumor and then image the left breast and axilla (armpit), marking the skin over the sites of lymph node activity.

"Some people say it hurts like hell and some don't feel much at all," she warned. After she injected the material, I informed her that I fell into the hurt-like-hell category. The good news is, thinking back on the experience of the entire day and post-operative period, that was the most uncomfortable part.

After a few minutes of being imaged under the camera, the tech looked at the screen and commented that several lymph nodes were lighting up. Apparently there were more showing up than usual, because she consulted with the radiologist.

"Not a problem," reassured Dr. Braitman. "It's not uncommon for several lymph nodes to be visualized by scintigraphy," she added as she marked my skin over the lymph node activity.

I was hot-wired, marked and ready. Next stop, outpatient surgery department. AJ and I were led into a small preparation room where a nurse started an IV in my right arm, after confirming that the surgery was to be on my left side. Dr. Schnaper then greeted us and reviewed the procedure and type of anesthesia I was to receive (IV sedation with a local). She went out and the anesthesiologist came in. I warned him that I was very sensitive to anesthetics, taking a long time to wake up after receiving general anesthesia in the past. Per Bonnie's advice, I asked for something to prevent post-op nausea.

Then it was my time. I was led on a gurney into the operating room and helped onto the OR table. I lay back and crossed my legs at the ankles. The last thing I remember is the anesthesiologist asking me to uncross them.

It was late afternoon when I woke up in Recovery. AJ was sitting beside me, and I could see the nurses at their station in front of me. The nurse tending to me noticed I was rousing, came over and asked how I was. Not too bad, just sleepy. Dr. Schnaper stopped by, relating that the biopsy had gone well and that four sentinel lymph nodes had been removed. Fortunately, I did not require any drains at the surgical sites. She reviewed the post-op instructions, warning me that my urine would look blue for a day or so from the lymph node dye she used. I was to call her office for a follow-up appointment on Friday.

After a few sips of water I was advanced to ginger ale. When I was sufficiently awake, the nurse removed the EKG monitor leads and my IV. Finally, I could get dressed. AJ helped me into Bonnie's red denim shirt, I slowly put on my jeans and slipped into clogs. He got the car and the nurse wheeled me out into the free world.

We arrived home at about six o'clock. Michael greeted us, attentively asking how I was.

"Pretty good, just tired," I replied.

I dozed in the bedroom upstairs while Michael and AJ ate dinner. AJ called my mother to let her know that all went well. By around nine o'clock, I'd slept enough. When AJ came to check on me, I was pleased to report that I felt comfortable and didn't need any pain medication.

A few minutes later the doorbell rang. Debbie had arrived! I heard AJ fill her in on the details of the day and how well I was feeling. She greeted Michael and they chatted about school. Then she came up to see me.

"Deb! I can't believe you're here! I'd like to hug you, but I'd better not," I laughed.

"How are you doing?" she inquired.

"Nothing hurts, and I'm not even that tired after the anesthesia." She sat on the edge of the bed and we caught up on things. I was comfortable and surrounded by people I loved. What could be bad?

3

The Results

Taijutsu, literally "the art of the body," refers to unarmed self-defense, the foundation of Ninjutsu, the martial art practiced by Ninjas. Steven Hayes describes taijutsu in terms of modes: earth, water, fire, wind, and void, which reflect the warrior's mindset.[1] Specific postures and directions of body movement characterize each of these.

When learning Ninjutsu, the first we studied as white belts was earth mode, used when there is a feeling of confidence, such as against a much smaller or less threatening attacker. It is embodied by an up and down motion, moving down as the strike or counterstrike is executed.

At orange belt level, we learned about water mode, in which a wave-like smooth angling back and forth motion is used to avert and then counterstrike an attack. At green belt it was fire mode. As the name implies, this is an aggressive, assertive means of attack or defense: you dare touch my kid and I'll go right through you with all my might. Purple belt techniques were in wind mode, with evasive, circular motions. Wind mode is used against someone who attacks and should be controlled or subdued, rather than disabled. At the highest level is the void, a creative flow of energy used in spontaneous self-defense. In this mode, reaction to an onslaught is unplanned, adapted to the energy and mood of the situation. Ready for the unexpected, one should not anticipate any particular attack, as this could limit the ability to respond.

I awoke on Halloween, relieved to have had a good night's sleep following surgery. I was comfortable, requiring no analgesics, not even Tylenol. The surgical dressing was well in place, and there had been no bleeding.

Debbie and I laughed a lot and lingered over our morning coffee. I told her in detail about the past eventful week.

I reviewed my mammogram with her, pointing out the microcalcifications. I then took out the x-ray of the biopsy specimen that Dr. Schnaper had removed. Specimen radiography is performed on the tissue excised after needle localization, to assure that the lesion identified on the mammogram has been totally removed. I agonized over the image with a magnifying glass, counting the calcifications on the mammogram and then comparing them to the x-ray of the specimen. I wanted to be sure every last one of the calcifications had been removed. Only a radiologist could torture herself to this extent! After several minutes, I was convinced that Dr. Schnaper had, indeed, removed the whole culprit. Three wires or not, that Dr. Munitz had done a good localization if the whole lesion had been removed.

What a treasure having my best friend there with me. As I still felt well after a couple of hours, we decided to go to the mall.

Debbie needed black pumps. I was not supposed to drive, but I navigated Deb to the Nordstrom's shoe department: Rachel and I loved the selection, and we always had fun trying on shoes. Deb and I spent so much time there, the salesmen came to know us by name. We ultimately wound up with just the shoes she was looking for. We then found cute pajamas for her 9-year-old daughter, Rebecca.

From the mall, we picked up Michael at school. Having recently received his learner's permit, he drove us home. I used the occasion of my recent surgery to emphasize the skills of smooth and steady starts and stops.

That evening, Debbie cooked us a delicious salmon dinner. We called her husband, Peter, and daughter Rebecca before they went out trick or treating. I thanked them for lending me Deb when I needed her. Michael set out five large bowls of Halloween candy, and we all sampled it, waiting for our trick or treaters. I could have been a Mummy for Halloween had Dr. Schnaper wrapped me head to toe.

Debbie was with me through the next afternoon and then flew back to New Hampshire. I tried to be sedentary much of the day, sitting at the computer, reading and petting the animals, my dog Meg and cats Gracie and Micetro. I was starting to receive wonderful cards in the mail, and it seemed every day there was another delivery of balloons or flowers. A huge balloon bouquet from people at work brightened my foyer. Flowers bedecked the kitchen and dining room, and my sister sent a cookie bouquet.

Thursday evening I was permitted to remove the surgical dressings. I was nervous: what if I didn't have a breast left? Slowly, I peeled off the bandages and held my breath. It didn't look bad at all! It was swollen under the armpit and at the surgical site. Other than that you could hardly tell-it still looked like a normal breast. Now THAT'S why you pick a good, experienced breast surgeon. Thank you, Dr. Schnaper!

Friday afternoon, AJ and I made the trek up to Dr. Schnaper's office again, this time for a post-op check and review of my results. She examined the surgical sites, which were beginning to heal.

After I dressed, AJ, Dr. Schnaper, and I sat in a small conference room. In great detail, writing important points down on a piece of paper for me as she went, Dr. Schnaper gave us the news. The tumor had been removed in its entirety and the margins around it were clear. (Yes!). It was estrogen and progesterone receptor positive, a good prognostic indicator. (Keep up the good news, Lauren!). Two other good prognostic indicators were the low proliferative activity marker, MIB-1, and the negative HER-2 *neu* status. HER-2 *neu*, she explained, is a human epidermal growth factor receptor which, when overexpressed (some of the DNA is more active than in normal tissue), indicates a more aggressive tumor. (So far so good!). Also, there were four sentinel lymph nodes removed. In two of the four, there was tumor identified only by immunohistochemical staining. This was a more rigorous means of finding individual tumor cells than the standard stains used. One lymph node contained 0.5 mm of tumor and the other, 1 mm. Based on that, it would be best for me to undergo chemotherapy, and I should follow-up with a medical oncologist. I already had an appointment with Dr. Minford for the following Tuesday. As I would be losing my hair, Dr. Schnaper advised that I cut it short now. Some of her patients had actually shaved their heads to lessen the trauma of hair loss.

We left her office in a state of shock. Chemotherapy?! Shaving my head? It all sounded so awful. Things were going from bad to worse. First I thought I'd just have DCIS. Then it turned out to be infiltrating ductal cancer. Now positive nodes and chemotherapy. I did not look forward to that at all. AJ somberly listened to my tirade. Two of his cousins had been through chemotherapy for breast cancer, and it was certainly no picnic. This was one time when it was difficult to think of anything reassuring to say.

When Michael got home from school, I broke the news to him.

"I've got good news and bad news," I told him.

"The bad news is that I've got to have chemotherapy," I continued, "but the good news is that you'll have one heck of a college essay."

"I've got it!" he said: "How My Mother and I Survived Her Cancer."

We had a guffaw over that one. The scary thing is some people might actually write it. We called Rachel with my latest development. Fortunately, she had a group of close friends, her "girls," as she called them, with whom she could share all the grim news I'd been phoning in. Michael's reaction was different. He did not mention it to his closest friends.

My next call was to Jessie. She and Jennifer were experts on chemotherapy. Jennifer had been through months of it following her brain cancer surgery. Jessie was full of practical suggestions for me, and I could hear Jennifer in the background chiming in advice. I took in every word. Both Jessie and Jennifer, with their strong, optimistic spirits and great senses of humor, were heroes to me.

"Let me give you the telephone number of Jennifer's acupuncturist," Jessie said.

Based on Jennifer's experience, I was very impressed with acupuncture. Jennifer had sustained bleeding at the site of her brain surgery, resulting in brainstem injury. She did not move or speak spontaneously for several months as a result. Jessie was constantly by her side in the hospital and then in the children's rehab center. At the advice of her husband's physician partner, Jessie called an acupuncturist. Shortly after beginning acupuncture, things turned around for Jennifer and she began moving and speaking again. She has made a steady, progressive recovery ever since.

I took the telephone number and told Jessie I would call as soon as I knew when I was to begin chemotherapy. I also mentioned to her that I'd had trouble eating and sleeping since all of this started.

"You should call Gordon," she advised. Gordon Livingston was the psychiatrist in our multispecialty group, whom I respected tremendously. That was my next phone call, and I managed to get an appointment for Tuesday, to follow my appointment with the oncologist. In retrospect, the timing was fortuitous.

I fully intended to do my usual announcing of the halftime show at the high school football game Saturday. I needed something else to think about, something other than cancer, something upbeat. It was so much fun watching Michael and Eric, the drum majors, leading the high school band and drill team onto the field before the game began.

Michael and Eric, along with the band director, Dr. VanDerBeek conducted "The Star Spangled Banner." AJ and I sat in the bleachers, watching the game and chatting with other parents around us. At five minutes before halftime, I climbed into the announcer's box, joining my neighbor, who did the commentary on the games and whose son was on the football team. I had the script that Michael and I had written:

"And now coming to you live, it's the Centennial High School Marching Unit....111 members strong, under the direction of Max VanDerBeek, assisted by drum majors Michael Alpert and Eric Trudel. Also presenting the Centennial High School Drill Team. The theme of the half-time show is "Funk." The marching unit will be performing the following numbers:

"What is Hip,"

"Boom Whacka Whacka Whacka Boom," which, as you might guess, stars the percussion section,

"All Things Bright and Beautiful," featuring the euphorious euphoniums, and

"You Dropped the Bomb on Me."

Bring it on, Band!

References:

1. Hayes, SK. *Enlightened Self-Protection: The Kasumi-An Ninja Arts Tradition.* Nine Gates Press, 1992, p.22.

4

Planning the Course

"When faced with multiple attackers," said Mr. Elrod, "be sure to keep moving so you line them up. Stay out of the center of the circle. Knock out the first and go after the rest." With your movement, you can line up your adversaries one behind the other, positioning one of them between you and the other attackers. "Zone your body so you're in control of the attack," advised Mrs. Elrod. Facing and looking directly at your attacker will make you a more intimidating adversary.

"You gain strength, courage and confidence by every experience in which you must stop and look fear in the face...You must do the thing that you think you cannot do."—Eleanor Roosevelt.

Election Day, 2000 was not only a fateful day for Al Gore and George W. Bush, although, come to think of it, it was more ambiguous than fateful for them at the time. AJ and I met with Dr. Jon Minford at 10 a.m. I was used to seeing Jon at conferences and committee meetings. In those settings, I appreciated his depth of knowledge, as well as his dry humor. He's a triathlete, and we would frequently discuss running and training for races.

I'd never seen Jon look so somber in all my life as when AJ and I were sitting across the desk from him. There I was, his colleague and a specialist in mammography, with a new diagnosis of breast cancer. As my college roommate put it, sometimes life just turns around and bites you in the ankle.

Jon looked over the pathology reports. At the viewbox in his office, I pointed out the cancer on my mammogram. He then went over to the white board alongside his desk and, illustrating with graphs and percentages, described to us in detail the survival benefits of chemotherapy for my Stage IIB breast cancer. The option of chemotherapy was a no-brainer for me: at 46 years old, I would go for every percentage point of survival I could get.

Because of the lymph node involvement, I was a candidate for aggressive chemotherapy: Cytoxan and Adriamycin for four cycles, followed by four cycles of Taxol. Each of the cycles of chemotherapy would occur three weeks apart, spanning a period of 24 weeks if all proceeded according to schedule. After a month off, I would undergo six to seven weeks of radiation therapy. Two weeks after completion of radiation therapy, I would begin taking Tamoxifen, a hormonal treatment, for five years. Whoa, that sounded like so much to go through.

> Note that dose dense chemotherapy, at two-week rather than three-week intervals is being increasingly used at the time of this writing. Also aromatase inhibitors, which block estrogen production in the body, now supplement tamoxifen in post-menopausal women with estrogen receptor positive tumors.

The first part of the discussion, statistics of my own mortality, was sobering enough. We then heard about the side effects of chemotherapy. I would lose my hair on day 17 after the first cycle of chemo. Day 17? Exactly day 17? How did he know that? Through experience. There are effects on the bone marrow: anemia, leukopenia (lowering of white blood cell counts), and attendant risks of infection.

Gastrointestinal side effects, that is, nausea, vomiting, and diarrhea, were common. Heartburn and a metallic taste in the mouth were additional side effects. Chemotherapy induces menopause in ninety percent of women my age. Adriamycin was potentially cardiotoxic, resulting in cardiomyopathy (heart muscle weakening) in a small percentage of patients. Taxol produced myalgias (muscle aches) and sometimes a reversible neuropathy (pins and needles sensation, particularly in the hands and feet), which was dose related.

Aggressive chemotherapy: it all sounded so scary and serious. I walked out of Jon's office holding six prescriptions. Six! I, who hesitated to take an Advil unless I was in agony, was going to fill six prescriptions. I wouldn't have to take them all, but they were good to have available in case I needed them.

First was Anzemet, for the prevention of nausea, to be taken on days 1, 2, and 3 after chemotherapy; Compazine pills and suppositories, for the treatment of nausea; Tequin, a strong, broad spectrum antibiotic; Zantac to be taken twice daily for heartburn; and Lorazepam for nausea/vomiting and anxiety. I should also have on hand the antacid of my choice, as well as Imodium A-D for the prevention of diarrhea.

My head was spinning. How did other patients, who were not in the medical field specializing in breast cancer and its detection, feel at this point? I couldn't imagine being any more overwhelmed than I was.

AJ left for work, and I met with Dr. Minford's nurse, who went over in detail the tests required prior to beginning chemotherapy. I would have to schedule an echocardiogram and a CT scan of the chest and abdomen. I would also need baseline bloodwork, including CBC (complete blood count), as well as liver, kidney, and electrolyte blood studies. So, in addition to the six prescriptions, I had labwork to be done and two tests to schedule. That was it. I was ready to see Gordon.

Gordon Livingston's office was so soothing: plants, dim lights, comfortable couch. He wasn't the type of psychiatrist who sat silently writing notes as the patient lay on a couch talking in a stream of consciousness gazing at the ceiling. Yes, I was on a couch, but sitting and facing him in his big desk chair. Gordon actually spoke and interacted, and even expressed an opinion once in awhile.

He began by asking me what was going on. When I told him I'd just been diagnosed with breast cancer, he immediately said: "I'm so sorry to hear that." I described the events of the past two weeks. While I was handling the situation adequately, I did notice trouble eating and sleeping. I mentioned the dreaded prospect of chemotherapy coming up in ten days. He asked about sources of support and if I believed in God. By the end of the hour, I felt better equipped to handle the situation. He prescribed me Zoloft, to ease some of my anxiety. At this point, I agreed it would be a good idea to try something like that. I would see him in two weeks, four days after my first chemotherapy treatment.

I started the Zoloft that very day. I'm so subject to the placebo effect: as a physician I know darn well that the therapeutic effect of the SSRI's (selective serotonin reuptake inhibitors, the class of drugs to which Zoloft belongs) takes about two to three weeks to kick in. I have such faith in modern medicine and ability to visualize beneficial effects that the very act of starting the Zoloft made me feel better. It's a good thing, too, because that night after dinner, Michael and I headed over to the Claudia Mayer Cancer Resource and Image Center by the hospital and went wig shopping. I was going to go alone, but Michael wanted to be sure I didn't pick out anything ridiculous looking, so he came along. Besides, this gave him another opportunity to practice driving.

The Claudia Mayer Center was only a few years old. It was named in memory of a local physician's wife who died of breast cancer at the age of 47. That struck a little close to home. Anyway, the facility is well done, including computers and an extensive library. In addition, there are salon stylists who donate their time to assist women in selecting and styling wigs. In another room, there is a selection of lingerie and prostheses for women who have undergone mastectomies. The selection of hats and scarves is enormous. There are also pillows and scented sachets that have been donated. I felt grateful to have access to a facility like this in my community.

Michael and I entered the wig room. I sat in the hair salon style chair while one of the stylists assisted me with my selections. She put a nylon cap over my hair for trying on the wigs, although I wouldn't need it once my hair was gone. The first I donned was a little redder than my natural color, but it was a fairly simple bob that I felt comfortable in. We then became a little more adventurous: I tried on a "boopsy" blonde wig, a brunette wig of big Texas hair, and a really short pixie cut, which I thought looked a bit too severe. We agreed that the first wig was the best, but it would have to be ordered in a color closer to my own auburn (otherwise, according to Michael, it looked like Ronald McDonald's hair).

The stylist left the room to get some hats and scarves. Michael took the opportunity to try on a big blond wig, throwing us into fits of hysterical laughter. We pulled it together in time for the stylist's return. She had both arms full of hats, turbans, and scarves.

"Turbans are nice for wearing around the house," she said. "You should consider getting some hats, if you just want to run out to the store and don't want to put on a wig." With winter coming up, I could do that and people wouldn't look at me twice. I wished I looked better in baseball caps, though.

By the time we walked out of the cancer resource center about an hour later, I had a large bag of hats and turbans. I would have to return in about a week for my wig, and I arranged to pick it up when a stylist would be there to trim it. Michael urged me to leave before I bought anything else. I had just enjoyed my first dose of "Retail" Therapy, the one type of therapy that Jon Minford hadn't told me about.

5

Getting Pumped

"Against two attacks: your partner will be coming at you with either two punches, two kicks, or a punch and a kick. What I want you to do," said Mrs. Elrod, "is to move out of the way of the first attack, and then defend against the second. I want to see good Tai sebaki (body movement). Remember to angle off the line of the attack to get out of the way." Timing and distance are critical. "This art is about timing, distance and balance," said Mr. Elrod; "I want to see your knees bent, with your shoulders balanced over your hips." One must cultivate a presence of mind and body, an awareness of oneself with respect to the surrounding environment. Movements should be fluid and relaxed, tensing up only at the moment of the strike.

I was a changed person when I returned to work on Wednesday, November 8. Accustomed to being on the giving rather that the receiving end of health care, I was now the doctor AND the patient. I resonated with a deeper empathy for my patients and knew firsthand the anxiety of the additional mammographic views after a screening study. I, too, had experienced the sleepless nights preceding a breast ultrasound and biopsy.

Donna and Bonnie our receptionists and Angie our health assistant greeted me warmly with hugs. Upon seeing me, Paul the team leader and MRI technologist said:

"Dr. Keen! It's great to see you again. How are you doing?"

"It feels so good to be back." I said. Susan, the mammo tech, came in, holding her cup of coffee.

"There she is," I exclaimed, "the woman who saved my life!"

"Oh come on," she said.

"Seriously," I continued, "if you hadn't gotten so far back on my mammogram, it would not have been found this early. And, I'll never accuse you of doing poor compression."

Anyone who thinks screening mammography doesn't affect mortality from breast cancer is mistaken.[1,2] If it weren't applied to women in their forties, I'd be, to put it bluntly, dead meat.

Sara from CT scan and Diana from ultrasound joined the welcome wagon. It was so good to be a normal person at work again. I told them I was to undergo chemotherapy, but I intended to continue working (God willing, I thought).

It was a hectic day of CT scans, ultrasounds, plain films, and mammograms. I was content to be busy, happy to jump back into my old life as though nothing had ever happened. I wish. The very nature of my work served as a constant reminder: follow-up mammogram on a woman twenty years after mastectomy for breast cancer (reassuring to see such a long term survivor); CT scan on a young woman with metastatic breast cancer (uh-oh). No doubt about it, I am here by the grace of God.

The following day I returned, once again embracing the workday. It was busy, and I could devote my thoughts to the patients and tasks at hand all day without self-absorption. I left by 5:45 pm for my 6 o'clock echocardiogram.

Back as a patient again, I lay on an ultrasound table. The technologist carefully scanned around the area of my recent surgery, angling in to visualize my heart. I watched the screen as she imaged the opening and closing valves and pumping chambers. That heart was doing a fine job, and I hoped the Adriamycin wouldn't interfere with it.

My last weekend before beginning chemotherapy was spent in preparation. I bought several books. One was *Dr. Susan Love's Breast Book*,[3] which I had often recommended to patients as a valuable resource on breast pathology and breast cancer treatments and their side effects. AJ's aunt had found Dr. Bernie Siegel's work inspirational for getting through her ovarian cancer chemotherapy. I purchased Dr. Siegel's book about exceptional cancer patients, *Love, Medicine and Miracles*,[4] as well as his tape, *Getting Ready: Preparing for Surgery, Chemotherapy, and Other Treatments*[5] to listen to during my chemotherapy.

AJ and I went to Sears, where he helped me select a ladies electric razor. Jessie had filled me in on some of the practical details about chemotherapy: who would have thought that you're not even supposed to shave your legs with a straight-edge razor because of the risk of getting cut and infected?

The next stop was my hairdresser Lisa's. I caught her up on what was happening with me. As suggested by Dr. Schnaper, I had my hair cut short, prior to starting chemotherapy. I wasn't sure if I wanted to shave my head after receiving the first chemo treatment. Lisa had done that for some of her clients in the past and gave me her home and cell phone numbers if I needed to call on short notice.

Saturday afternoon was my first acupuncture session. The office, in a low brick building, was in a serene setting nestled in the woods. I walked into an intimate waiting room, decorated with oriental artwork. Classical music was playing from a boom box on the desk.

Sandy Johnson emerged from one of the four treatment rooms and greeted me with a warm smile. I remember having met Sandy for the first time at Jennifer's bedside, where Sandy was administering a treatment. The changes that occurred after Jennifer began acupuncture! To go from the locked-in brainstem syndrome of not moving and speaking for several months to speech and movement was nothing short of a miracle.

Sandy led me to one of the treatment rooms, a cozy room with a desk, two chairs and the treatment table, a table with a mattress and sheet on it. Charts of the acupuncture meridians over the human body hung on the walls. Sandy took a detailed medical history from me, with emphasis on the most recent events. I mentioned how I'd felt a knot in my stomach since all of this had begun.

She, herself, was a breast cancer survivor of seven years. Sandy recalled that when she was diagnosed, one of the most important things her doctor did was to look her right in the eye and say:

"There is nothing you did that caused you to get breast cancer."

Those words rang through my mind. All the what if's I'd been putting myself through! What if I had been a vegetarian? What if I hadn't taken the pill? What if I hadn't grown up on Long Island?

We don't yet know the cause or causes of breast cancer at this point. Mammography is the best although not perfect tool for early detection, which results in improved survival, not to mention the need for less drastic surgery. There has been such a proliferation of books about the unproven, things you can do or eat to prevent breast cancer, yet the proven benefits of mammography are in dispute. Go figure.

For a physical exam, Sandy looked at my tongue and felt my pulses. She didn't just feel my radial arteries (at the wrists) to check for a pulse rate like I do. Sandy felt each radial artery in three different spots and at two different depths, to evaluate the flow of energy, "Qi," through each of the twelve meridians of my body. This was a totally different concept of the human body in health and disease than I learned in medical school. Acupuncture treats the bodymindspirit as if it's all one, not the specialized compartments that I'm accustomed to in my Western medical training.

We talked about visualization and a positive attitude in approaching cancer treatment. In his book, Bernie Siegel mentioned using imagery and visualization with his cancer patients. Athletes and musicians use visualization to improve their performance. I had read that positive attitude can improve outcome and survival. I was going for every percentage point of survival I could get, and if positive attitude improved it, I was going to have one. At 46 years old, with two wonderful children and a great husband, I was determined to survive a long time.

Sandy began by treating my stress with "the Four Gates," that is, one acupuncture point in each of my hands and feet. She noted that often, for a first acupuncture treatment, AE (aggressive energy) points were needled. Based on my pulses, AE would not be a treatment necessary for me at this time.

The acupuncture needles were small and threadlike. They didn't particularly hurt when inserted, but I could feel a distinct tingling sensation when the correct point was hit. Each acupuncture point is precisely determined by the relationship to surrounding anatomic structures. Sandy feels for the energy of the point itself. Sometimes, she says, she can even see the energy. In addition to treating me for stress, Sandy began preparing me for chemotherapy. Among other points she needled "Stomach 36," a point in my left shin, and "Pericardium 6" in my wrists to minimize the nausea-inducing effects.

As I lay on the acupuncture table, I consciously used visualization of the upcoming chemotherapy. Enough anticipating side effects. I was to undergo chemotherapy to cleanse my body of any cancer cells that were in it. While I was pretty certain that Dr. Schnaper had gotten them all with the negative margins at the tumor site and only two of four sentinel nodes with micrometastases, the purpose of the chemotherapy was to rinse my body of any other dysplastic or neoplastic cells that dared reside anywhere within me.

I imagined every cell of my body being scrubbed clean. The imagery I used was what was familiar to me, what I could relate to. Nothing fancy. My cells were laundry in the washer, i.e., the chemotherapy, followed by the dryer, i.e., radiation therapy. Or, I thought, it was like going to the hairdresser: first the shampoo (chemotherapy), followed by the cut (hair loss), and finishing up with the hairdryer (radiation). I lay there in stream of consciousness, focusing on positive associations for chemotherapy, all the good things it would do for my body and ultimately my survival.

When I arose from the acupuncture table one hour later, I felt incredibly relaxed. I had a sense of release, the relief you get after a good cry. The knot in my stomach had been untied.

Sunday afternoon I heard from my friend Sandie Isbister. She was a radiologist who had worked with Jessie and me, and was now in a practice doing ultrasound. We chatted about our children and their activities. Her son had just started Swarthmore, which was exciting, but plenty of work. Her daughter attended a private high school. Then I shared my news, including my imminent chemo.

"Do you know of a good acupuncturist?" she asked. Sandie, while schooled in Western medicine, had been helped by complementary medicine, including acupuncture.

"Oh, yes," I replied. "I went to see Jennifer's acupuncturist yesterday! It was so relaxing. I felt much better afterwards."

The next morning, AJ drove me to my office for the CT scan of my chest and abdomen. I had taken 25 mg. of Benadryl one hour before to relax me and prevent any contrast reaction. I had never had intravenous contrast before, and this was not the standard pretreatment for people with contrast allergy, but I figured a little Benadryl wouldn't hurt and could possibly help. As a result, the CT scan felt quite relaxing.

I drank a cup of barium one hour before and another as I sat on the CT scan table.

"Sara, you're a good cook! I don't know what those patients are complaining about," I said. "If I ever get hungry at work, I'll have to come get some."

Sara positioned me on the CT table and began looking for a vein to place my IV. I could tell she was apprehensive about getting a good stick on her doctor, but I had a cooperative vein in my right antecubital fossa (elbow crease), and the IV went right in. I could feel the slightly cool fluid flow through my arm veins during the scan. After a couple of minutes, I had a sensation of warmth, as if I had just drunk a glass of wine, a common sensation after intravenous contrast is administered.

Sara asked me to hold my breath for each scan. The trick was to try and make each breath the same depth. I spent the whole scan thinking about getting my breathing right, and before I knew it, it was over.

There are some perks to being in the field. Jessie and I looked over the scan right away, and I knew when I walked out of my office that my chest and abdomen were free of metastases. Thank God! There were fluid collections at the surgical sites in the left breast and axilla (armpit). Jessie and the technologist, Diana, did an ultrasound to obtain accurate measurements of them. Pretty sizable: the one in the breast measured about 6 cm. (over 2 inches) and that in the armpit was 4 cm (a bit over 1 ½ inches) in diameter.

Tuesday was my bone scan. I drove myself, since I hadn't taken any premedication for it. The nuclear medicine office was only a mile from my house. I was injected with the radiopharmaceutical and then had to return two hours later for my images. The technologists recognized me from my working in that office. One of them was, herself, battling metastatic breast cancer. They apologized about how close the scanning camera had to be. I had to lie perfectly still for several minutes as I was being scanned. I didn't see what there was to apologize about. Lying there on a table in a sunny room on a beautiful autumn day: this had to be the most pleasant of all the procedures I'd been through. I was able to look at the images when my exam was completed. Thankfully, the only "hot spot" that showed up was in my big toe, just a little arthritis. Yay, no metastases!

The next stop was the Claudia Mayer Center, to pick up my new wig. I tried it on, and a hairdresser volunteering at the center trimmed it up for me. I had never before realized that a wig required trimming. Of course, I'd never owned a wig before, either. The stylist was an Italian gentleman who clipped the wig with panache and spoke about how much he loved his work. He complimented my choice of wig for my features. I was feeling quite good about myself by the time I left.

I brought the wig and a wig stand home and set it up on the bathroom counter, all ready for when I'd need it on day 17 of my chemotherapy cycle. My dog Meg entered the room to greet me. Then she stopped in her tracks: she'd caught site of the new furry dark creature and began to bark.

My pre-chemo appointment with Jon Minford was later that afternoon. I would be getting the standard treatment of 4 cycles of Cytoxan/Adriamycin at three-week intervals, followed by 4 cycles of Taxol, also three weeks apart, assuming my counts cooperated. It is common, he warned, to have to delay at least one of the cycles due to low counts.

Jon reviewed my nutritional requirements on chemotherapy: I should increase my protein intake and be sure to drink plenty of water. No alcohol. Avoid herbal supplements. I could continue to exercise to the extent I felt comfortable, although he didn't recommend sparring in karate at this time. My blood counts (red cells, white cells, and platelets) would go down between days 10 and 14 of the chemotherapy cycle. I should be particularly careful to avoid crowds and exposure to people at that time.

I needed to take my temperature daily at about 5 p.m. and rinse my mouth with a solution of 1 teaspoon of baking soda in a cup of water 4 to 6 times a day, to reduce the risk of infection. (I wasn't sure how I'd manage that one at work).

My veins looked good, so I would not need a surgically placed port for IV access at this time. Yes! Another surgery averted! I was scheduled for my first chemotherapy session Friday, November 17, not even a month after my initial screening mammogram.

Okay, Jon, I'm scanned, rested, and ready. Let the chemo begin.

References:

1. Tabar L, Yen MF, Vitak B, et al. Mammography service screening and mortality in breast cancer patients: 20-year follow-up before and after introduction of screening. Lancet 2003;361:1405-1410.

2. Smith RA, Saslow D, Sawyer KA, et al. American Cancer Society Guidelines For breast cancer screening: update 2003. CA Cancer J Clin 2003;53:141-169.

3. Love, SM. *Dr. Susan Love's Breast Book.* Perseus Publishing, 2000.

4. Siegel, BS. *Love, Medicine and Miracles: Lessons Learned About Self Healing from a Surgeon's Experience with Exceptional Patients.* Harper Perennial 1998.

5. Siegel, BS. *Getting Ready: Preparing for Surgery Chemotherapy, and Other Treatments (Audiocassette).* Hay House Audio 1999.

6

Initiation

"Use your attacker's energy," advised Mrs. Elrod. "Against a grab and a push," she continued, "move back with the attack and throw your opponent with a side sacrifice throw, dropping down right in front of his leg. Your partner's energy is already moving forward and he'll drop downward". Or, if your opponent grabs and pulls you, move forward with the attack, loosen up your partner with a hit, and then turn and throw him in a gansakanage, literally "throwing a big rock." When I'm the attacker and my partner captures my energy for the gansakanage, I have the sensation of being in a whirlpool, going down the drain. Use the energy of the attack. Go with the flow.

"If you flow with the fight, being flexible to the opponent's attack and changing position, you will never be defeated."—Grandmaster Masaaki Hatsumi.[1]

Chemotherapy. Just the word sends chills down your spine: images of harsh substances with names like nitrogen mustard coursing through peoples' veins, causing toxic side effects such as nausea, vomiting, and baldness. Well, forget those images. Chemotherapy is no big deal. I've been through it, nothing awful happened to me, and I'm here on the other side of it to tell you that, I repeat, chemotherapy is no big deal.

I was all ready for my first chemotherapy session. I had packed a small tote bag with Michael's portable tape recorder and my Bernie Siegel tapes and book. Guess I wouldn't need a bag lunch for this event, though.

Jon Minford had recommended that I drink green tea at breakfast. Some of his patients had told him that it helped settle their stomachs. I drank a cup of green tea and ate a bowl of oatmeal for breakfast, something to "stick to my ribs" and hopefully not wind up anywhere else.

AJ was very quiet driving me to the outpatient oncology center on Friday, November 17, 2000. He was remembering two of his cousins who had been through chemotherapy for breast cancer and experienced adverse side effects. I said that I just wanted to start already to get the whole thing over with sooner.

We checked in at the nurses' station. The receptionist Terry and nurses recognized my name from radiology reports on their patients over the years. As AJ and I were signing me in, my friend and radiologist colleague Sandie showed up, holding a bouquet of flowers. Angel of mercy, she had come to sit by me during my chemotherapy session! We shooed AJ away to work. I would call him in about 2 hours to pick me up.

One of the nurses Patty took Sandie and me back to the chemotherapy suite: a big room with eight cushiony recliners. It was a corner room, with windows on two sides, looking out to the surrounding woods. Not a bad view. There was only one other patient there at the time, an elderly gentleman, so I just about had my pick of seats. A few other patients and their families arrived later in the morning during the course of my infusion.

It wasn't a frightening place at all, but everyone seemed so somber. Sandie and I would have none of that. We sat talking as if it were over lunch. Never mind the IV poles attached to the people in the easy chairs. Choosing to be oblivious to the sedate atmosphere, we laughed about our kids' antics and activities and discussed our careers. Our contagious good cheer brightened the surroundings. The woman next to us, initially hovering over her dozing husband at the end of an IV, joined us in conversation, momentarily distracted from her troubles.

First Patty described what was about to happen: she would start the IV, put in premedications, and then run the chemo. Since my surgery had been on the left side, she started the IV in a large vein in my right forearm. I appreciated Patty's expertise, getting the IV in right away with no difficulty. The cool fluid began to flow through my arm.

My premedications consisted of Atavan (an anxiety-reducing medication), Dexamethasone (a steroid to reduce the risk of allergic reaction) and Anzemet (an antiemetic). Within minutes I felt drowsy, with a mild buzz. Patty came by with a big syringe loaded with red fluid. This was the Adriamycin, to be administered slowly over the course of 15 minutes by hand injection, alternating via a three-way stopcock with another syringe of saline, to minimize the irritating effects on the vein.

"It's such a pretty color," I commented, trying to make the best of the situation.

Next came the Cytoxan dripped in from a small IV bag of fluid over the course of about 45 minutes. Sandie and I continued our conversation, unphased by it all.

And then it was done. My first chemotherapy treatment was over! One down, three more Cytoxan/Adriamycins and four more Taxols to go. I called AJ to come for me.

Patty and I went over a calendar she had made for me, marking the date and each day of my chemotherapy cycle. There was even a turkey drawn in on Thanksgiving Day. On days 8 and 21, I was to get blood drawn to check my counts (red cells, white cells, and platelets). I scheduled an appointment with Dr. Minford for day 12. She placed the calendar in a red folder, along with patient information sheets about Cytoxan and Adriamycin and when it would be necessary to call Dr. Minford's office (temperature over 100.4 degrees, uncontrollable nausea or vomiting, and a list of other gruesome what-if's).

When AJ arrived a few minutes later he was quite solicitous.

"How did it go?" he asked anxiously.

"Fine," I reassured him. "Sandie and I chatted the whole time. And look at these flowers she brought me!" He held my arm gently as we walked to the car, although I felt quite well and steady on my feet. In ten minutes we were home. I told him to go on back to work.

"Okay," he said incredulously, "if you're sure you're all right." Once he left, I looked through the literature Patty had given me about the medications I'd just received. Not very encouraging reading, mentioning all sorts of possible side effects. I took a look in Susan Love's book for another perspective. Oh, another side effect I hadn't known about: chemo brain. Chemo brain? Cognitive impairment, mild memory loss. I didn't want that one either.

I decided to stop reading about the chemotherapy, and indulge myself in something I never did: watch daytime television. By the time Michael got home from school, I was happily ensconced on the couch watching "the Rosie O'Donnell Show." He hesitantly asked how I was, and I told him that I felt fine, just a bit tired from the premedications I had been given. He plopped down beside me and watched TV with me before starting his homework.

I noticed a bit of a metallic taste in my mouth in the evening, but that was about it. I slept 11 hours that night! The next morning, although not feeling nauseous, I decided I would follow what Dr. Minford prescribed and take the Anzemet (anti-emetic) to prevent anything from happening. As it could cause drowsiness, I could not drive while taking it. Michael drove when we went to his All-State orchestra audition in the morning. I was thankful to be feeling well enough to accompany him, as it was our tradition to have me go along with him.

In the afternoon, AJ drove me to my second acupuncture session. I mentioned the fluid collections at the surgical sites in my breast and axilla. Sandy did points in my extremities to "move the fluid around," and she again treated "Stomach 36" and "Pericardium 6" to prevent nausea.

Acupuncture isn't just about treating symptoms by directing needles to a point here and a point there. It's based on maintaining a balanced flow of energy, "Qi," throughout the body. Sandy felt my pulses and treated accordingly. Again, I used the time to focus on the cleansing, therapeutic effects of the chemotherapy I was receiving. This is like a pregnancy, I thought. I will emerge from this treatment cleansed, renewed, reborn.

I had started keeping a journal after the first reeling week following my mammogram. Writing down the recent events helped me sort out some of the confusion and myriad feelings. My journal entry for 11/18/00:

That which doesn't kill you makes you stronger.

I was going to be mighty powerful by the end of all this.

Before dinner, AJ and I went to the gym. On the Stairclimber I felt so thankful and amazed to be there. AJ, Michael and I went out for Mexican food. I found the spicy salsa particularly appealing, as it overcame the mild metallic taste in my mouth. My appetite was undaunted!

All weekend, AJ kept looking at me expectantly, waiting for something awful to happen.

"I really feel okay," I reassured him. "Well," I continued, "maybe I do get tired 9:30 at night, but otherwise I'm okay."

AJ picked up Rachel from the airport on Sunday. She'd flown home directly from Boston, flush with Yale's football victory over Harvard. Normally, I would have accompanied him to pick her up, but we agreed it would be a better idea for me to stay put. I had taken the Anzemet as instructed on day 2 of the chemotherapy cycle, which left me a bit drowsy.

This was the first time Rachel and I had seen each other since Parents' Weekend and the onset of all of my medical adventures. She gave me a big hug and was reassured to see me looking like my usual self. In keeping with our tradition of baking together, we soon started a batch of blondies.

"The only bad thing about chemo," I said, "is that I can't eat the raw cookie dough."

"Michael and I will have to take care of it," Rachel assured me.

The calls kept coming in. My brother and sister, Wayne and Leslie, were so attentive. They both called to see how my first chemo session went. I was wondering whether or not I should shave my head, as Dr. Schnaper had suggested. Wayne, a hairdresser, said that some of his clients did not lose their hair after chemotherapy for breast cancer. While Jon Minford seemed fairly certain that I would, what if I were one of the few who didn't? After all, I felt pretty normal after the first treatment. My sister, true New Yorker that she is, put it bluntly:

"What if you're not going to lose your hair? Shmuck!" We laughed heartily at that, but she had a good point. I decided that I would not shave my head, but just clip my hair short.

On Monday, I felt well and decided not to take the Anzemet, as it made me drowsy. I took it easy, reading, hanging out with Rachel. A new outlet mall not too far from us was having a grand opening. This was one event Rachel and I would have loved to go to together, but on the chemo I was to avoid crowds. That Retail Therapy would have to wait. Rachel went with one of her friends to check it out.

In the early afternoon, I went out to satisfy my craving for a Burger King Whopper. That evening, Rachel, Michael and I attended karate class. Per Jon Minford's instructions, I avoided the sparring, although I was able to participate in the bagwork and katas.

When I saw Gordon my psychiatrist the following day, we discussed my first chemotherapy treatment (so far so good) and what I'd been reading about the subject. He suggested I consult the Internet for additional resources and chat rooms. I took his advice and sat down at the computer when I returned home. I came upon two informative websites that I particularly liked. One was the site of the Susan G. Komen Foundation, www.komen.org, and the other, www.breastcancer.org. The chat rooms I visited were not helpful to me at that point. Since the time of my treatment I have learned about another website, www.comedycures.org. It offers humorous respite from the gravity of chronic illness. Fortunately, I had Michael around for my comic relief.

I was a little anxious about going to work on Wednesday. Would I be able to handle it? Would I tire easily? Fortunately, my fears were not realized. I was able to keep up the pace just fine. Contact with patients energized me. The staff and technologists were wonderful, asking to do anything to help, offering me cups of water, insisting I sit. All were amazed at how well I felt. I thought to myself thank God for giving me the strength and well-being to be able to continue serving my patients.

"Life is not easy for any of us. But what of that? We must have perseverance and above all confidence in ourselves. We must believe that we are gifted for something and that this thing must be attained."—Marie Sklodowska Curie.[2]

Thursday was Thanksgiving. The four of us packed into our car and drove the 3 hours to AJ's parents' home for a quiet Thanksgiving dinner. They usually invited extended family and many friends to their home for the occasion. In my honor, they kept the number of people down to limit my exposure to crowds. In addition to AJ, Rachel, Michael, and me, there were AJ's parents, Nana Joan and Papa Bob, and his older brother Jonny with his wife Keiko, who drove in from New York City, and their daughter, Tami, who had flown in from her job in California.

We arrived in the late afternoon, to a fanfare of Jonny's barking dogs. Everyone was gathered in the kitchen, talking all at once and making preparations for the feast. Tami had baked her first pumpkin pie from real, not canned, pumpkin. Keiko was creating a magnificent salad of exotic fruits, and Nana was tending the enormous turkey.

Everyone was quite solicitous of me. I told them I was feeling well, but just needed more sleep lately. They looked at me in astonishment—the same look that AJ had given me the weekend before, after my first chemotherapy session, waiting for something to happen.

When I asked Papa how he was feeling, he laughed and said, "Don't ask." He himself was struggling with his health. He had been afflicted with a progressive peripheral neuropathy for ten years. Most people by this time would have been confined to a wheelchair, but he was determined to persevere and do as much as he could on his own. Thus he went to the gym two to three times a week to work with a physical therapist, training with weights to maintain as much strength as possible, which meant that his strength was declining more slowly than in the typical course of the disease. Though unsteady on his feet, he insisted on walking when he could, balancing himself with a cane. Certainly, my own ailments seemed minor by comparison, but I intended to learn from and emulate his spirit and determination.

We sat down to a wonderful feast. Papa Bob always began the festivities with a toast:

"We appreciate being here together. The difficulties some of us have faced lead us to value this reunion all the more."

"L'Chayim," Nana chimed in.

"L'Chayim!" we echoed, clinking our glasses.

References:

1. Hatsumi, Masaaki. *Ninpo: Wisdom for Life*. Kihon Press, 2002, p.93-94.

2. Kuligowska E. Marie Sklodowska Curie: Inspirational Role Model and Mother of Science 1867-1934. Journal of Women's Imaging 2003;5:68-73.

7

Look Ma No Hair

"Today we'll be working on defenses against the wall," said Mrs. Elrod. "Your opponent has you pushed with your back against the wall in a lapel grab, preparing to punch with the other arm. A technique to use in defense is the Temakra, the 'pillow throw.' Place your hand on your partner's hand that's grabbing your lapel. With the other hand, counterstrike the punch coming in and then lock your attacker's elbow, turning to slam your opponent into the wall." Even when your back is up against the wall keep fighting. In the words of Winston Churchill:
"Never, never, never quit."

While I ran out of steam earlier at night, I was still able to maintain my daily activities. The week after Thanksgiving, I went to the gym on my typical Tuesday schedule. I was up to doing my usual routine on the weights and Stairclimber.

Coincidentally, I ran into one of the oncology nurses from the hospital, whom I'd known from the cancer committee. I greeted her as we were side by side on leg machines. After talking a few minutes, I told her that I was on chemotherapy for breast cancer and had just completed my first cycle of Cytoxan and Adriamycin.

She noted how much better the treatment and antiemetics are currently than when she first started oncology nursing. Chemotherapy patients used to require hospitalization because they became so sick. I wondered to myself if that's what it had been like for my father during his unsuccessful battle with Hodgkin's lymphoma forty years ago.

I brought up the hair issue. While seemingly a superficial thing, losing all your hair on chemotherapy is no small matter, and it was on my mind.

"My hair hasn't started falling out yet," I noted hopefully. Unfortunately, she seemed fairly certain that it would.

Later that day at acupuncture I told Sandy in amazement that the fluid collections in my left breast and axilla had resolved. Unbelievable. I've seen them take weeks or even months to go away in patients. Acupuncture sure moved the fluid out of there quickly, but thinking of Jessie's daughter Jennifer, I commented that it wasn't the first time I'd seen miracles with acupuncture!

I did notice some numbness in my skin at the surgical sites, although Dr. Schnaper had mentioned that she cut some cutaneous nerves getting to the sentinel lymph nodes. A little numbness was nothing to complain about.

I used my time on the acupuncture table to visualize (cleanotherapy, strength, resilience) and to reflect. Why does it take getting cancer to learn to take care of ourselves, value our lives, and appreciate each day?

It was good to get back to work the rest of the week. At the mammography center, I felt I was meant to be there, reading mammograms and doing biopsies. What a privilege to be a physician. I could speak to my patients with knowledge of breast cancer from the doctor's and the patient's vantage points.

Over the weekend, I began to notice some hair loss. I decided that Sunday, day 16 of my first chemotherapy cycle, would be the day for AJ to cut my hair really short to ease the trauma of losing it. I asked if it would bother him and if I should have the hairdresser do it, but AJ didn't seem to mind. Very businesslike, he took our barber scissors and chopped away, leaving me with hair about the length of his. I had read about women on chemotherapy losing their hair all over their pillows at night, so I decided to sleep in one of the turbans I'd bought from the cancer resource center, just in case.

I awoke on Day 17 not quite sure what to expect. Would all my hair suddenly be gone? It was still there. Michael stroked my hair and commented that I was shedding, like the cats do in the summertime. I did notice more hair than usual in the drain after the shower.

The hair loss occurred not over the course of one day but over a week, in a steady flurry of shedding. I began wearing the wig to work that week. Michael and I thought it appropriate to name the wig: Doris. It just seemed to fit her neat, short bobbed appearance. Hello, Doris!

I did not feel particularly ill after chemotherapy, but seeing myself in the mirror with no hair, I knew I was a cancer patient. I was grateful to Doris for helping me out in the outside world, where others would not have to know unless I chose to tell them. There could be no hiding it from me!

AJ, Doris, and I went to Michael's orchestra winter concert in early December. I was happy to be out in public, listening to the music, appreciating being alive and feeling well. Several of Michael's friends' parents complimented me on my new hairstyle. That's one thing I liked about Doris—never a bad hair day. I've come out of the experience feeling that any hair day is a good hair day.

I met with Jon Minford on Tues., Dec. 5. I told him I felt well and had only taken the Anzemet on days 1 and 2 of the cycle to prevent any nausea. I reported my need to sleep more: 11 hours/night the first several days after chemo, and subsequently 9 hours/night. Going to the gym kept my energy level up, and I could still do the same amount of weights, with a little more rest between sets. And, I'd been good; I didn't spar in karate. Thankfully, my blood counts were holding up, so I was good to go for cycle number two that Friday.

Sandie phoned Thursday night to be sure my chemo was on schedule. Friday morning I dined on oatmeal and green tea, since it had sat well with me the first time. AJ dropped me off for the treatment. He was feeling a little more sanguine, since I'd gone through the first one without incident.

I signed in and Patty took me back to the treatment room. As she prepared to start the IV, I pointed out a sclerosed (clotted off) vein in my forearm, resulting from my first treatment. Fortunately, there were still several others to choose from.

Sandie arrived a few minutes into my pretreatment medications. It was good to have this time to catch up with each other's lives. She was crocheting a scarf for her son and worked on it while chatting with me. Sandie used a big gauge crochet hook and beautiful thick, soft chenille wool in deep rich colors.

"It goes faster that way. I can finish a scarf in no time at all," she commented.

"I used to like to crochet," I told her. "Maybe I'll take it up again now that I should be resting a little more."

Sandie also brought me little gifts to keep my spirits up: a lavender scented pillow and a small inspirational book of biblical psalms and proverbs with a beautiful bookmark that she had crafted.

The Woman of Valor
Proverbs 31

The woman of valor: A priceless find,
    A treasure more precious than pearls.
An unfailing asset to her husband,
    She assures him a life of contentment.
Eager, energetic, far-sighted, and strong,
    Her family knows she will always be near.
Her optimism never wavers,
    Her industriousness never flags.

She extends a hand to the poor;
> She offers her hands to the needy.

She projects strength and dignity,
> And is confident about the future.

Her speech abounds with wisdom;
> She soothes everyone with words of kindness.

Her children bring her fulfillment,
> Her husband sings her virtues:

"Many women have excelled,
> but you surpass them all."

Charm is a mask and beauty is vain,
> But a righteous woman is deserving of praise

Her handiwork attests to her merit;
> All her actions bring her honor.

8

Round Two

"This is Basics Week," said Mrs. Elrod. "We'll be starting out with bagwork. First practice your punches: straight punches, jabs, uppercuts, and also elbow strikes. I want to see good taijutsu. Keep your knees bent and move your whole body as you punch. Punch not just with your arms, but from your hips, pivoting them with each strike."

We went on to practice kicks on the bag: front snap kicks, heel stomps, sidekicks, round kicks, knee strikes.

"Remember to follow through on the kicks; put your whole body into it," instructed Mrs. Elrod. "On the heel stomp kicks, bring your knee up to your chest for greater power."

Concentrating intently on the movements, you can feel when the punch or kick is well executed: an effortless relaxed flow of energy transmitted from your body to the bag. After class, Mr. and Mrs. Elrod presented me with an exquisite glass angel bell. It sits on my bureau watching over me to this day.

I looked out the large window in the acupuncture room as I lay on the table during my treatment. The leaves had almost completely fallen from the trees.

"When those leaves start growing back, so will my hair," I thought. As Dianne Connelly described in her book *Traditional Acupuncture: The Law of the Five Elements*:

"We are the seasons. We are the Elements. Nature is without and within us, each of us every moment. We are a replica of the universe passing from season to season in a natural unending cycle of life."[1]

The acupuncture session was on the day following my second cycle of Cytoxan/Adriamycin. I was glad to be halfway through with that combo! I had taken Anzemet to ward off any nausea, so AJ had to drive me to my treatment.

At home I indulged in being a couch potato. While AJ prepared dinner, I watched cooking shows and slept in front of the television. The love for food and its preparation pervades my family, and I'm convinced that it facilitated my getting through chemotherapy.

While my appetite wasn't at its best, I still enjoyed eating. My taste for spicy food was heightened, to mask the slightly metallic taste I felt the first week after chemotherapy. Thanks to the Zantac (which decreased gastric acid production), I was able to indulge my tastes without the heartburn I normally would have gotten!

Getting adequate rest and regular acupuncture, I felt that I was caring for myself better than I'd ever done before. When I dropped by the office to bring Jessie her birthday gift, she said I looked more rested than usual. I had come to appreciate my body, viewing good health as something to cherish. While I continued to exercise regularly and as much as I safely could, gone were the days of pushing myself to the limits of overwork, sleep deprivation and taking my body for granted. In that way, I actually felt better on chemotherapy than before!

I was more fatigued on the first two and a half days after this cycle of chemotherapy compared to the first. I again slept 11-12 hours the first few nights, getting to bed by 9:30. By Monday afternoon, though, I was feeling more energetic. I went to the gym and then rewarded myself with the Burger King Whopper that I had again been craving. I don't know what it is about Cytoxan and Adriamycin that made me go for those Whoppers, but they sure hit the spot.

I then headed over to the craft store to buy crocheting supplies. I purchased a large size (P) crochet hook and several skeins of thick chenille wool in a deep purple to make a hat and scarf set for Rachel. When Michael came home from school, I was engrossed in counting stitches to keep the gauge even on Rachel's scarf.

"Next you should make me an Afghan," suggested Michael.

"That's a great idea. It will go really fast with this large hook and this soft, thick wool," I said.

I had another session with my colleague and psychiatrist Gordon on Tuesday. I was feeling well enough to be more upset about the protracted presidential election results than about my own physical condition, a good sign. But the hair loss is no small matter and we talked about that. I was wearing my wig at the time. As he has a good sense of humor, I knew I could tell him we named it Doris without fear of getting committed.

I was conscious of setting a good example for my children in dealing with adversity and was determined to accept my situation rather than mope about it. In the words of Eleanor Roosevelt:

"You have to accept whatever comes and the only important thing is that you meet it with courage and the best you have to give."

Even the baldness had a good side. I calculated the time saved getting ready for work in the morning. Not having to style my hair: 10 minutes a day! That's over an hour a week and more than two days a year! AJ took the baldness as a sign that the chemotherapy was working, since I was feeling so well otherwise. Michael liked to admire my bald head and kiss it for luck.

Rachel came home from school the following week, having completed her finals for the semester. She would be home only a few days before her trip to Israel. I told her that when she was ready, I would show her how I looked without hair. I knew it would take some preparation. Rachel was relieved to see me looking otherwise healthy and in my usual good spirits.

"Rache, I've got an indomitable spirit," I told her.

"What's that?" she inquired.

"Indomitable means it can't be stopped, it's unbeatable, and this is not going to beat it!" The next day, Rachel's curiosity got the better of her, and she asked to see my head. We went into the large master bathroom.

"Ok, are you ready?" I asked.

"I guess so," she said. I took off the winter cap I was wearing.

"There are a few wisps of hair still left in the front, just like a baby's head," I said.

"Okay, I've seen enough," Rachel replied.

"It takes some getting used to," I told her, as I put my hat back on. A couple of days later, Rachel came into my bedroom as I was getting ready. She was holding her baby hairbrush and a tiny butterfly barrette that I had given her about ten years before. It had been mine when I was in first grade. The baby brush was perfect for the down I had left.

"You can use this barrette for the wisps of hair in front," she said. We went to the mirror, and I was able to clasp the butterfly around several of the hairs.

"I like the look," I remarked.

A few days later, wearing the purple crocheted scarf I had just completed, Rachel went back up to New Haven to meet the rest of the group from her school going on the trip to Israel. It was only a twelve day trip but would be packed with touring and activities.

"I wouldn't normally say this," I started, "but, put in a good word for me at the Western Wall."

References:

1. Connelly, Diane M. *Traditional Acupuncture: The Law of the Five Elements.* Traditional Acupuncture Institute, Columbia, MD, 1994, p.11.

9

Mama's Here for You

Mr. and Mrs. Elrod's teacher Mr. Bud Malmstrom came up from Georgia to give a seminar on protecting others. Sensei Malmstrom has attained the highest level, 10th degree black belt, in the art of Bujinkan Ninpo Taijutsu. A former marine, he currently works in law enforcement in Georgia and teaches martial arts. He speaks from practical experience.

Mr. Malmstrom discussed techniques used in executive protection. The point is to protect someone, the principal, as unobtrusively as possible and without disturbing him. The first technique demonstrated was the seemingly simple act of stepping in the way of an approaching individual, without the principal having to change his gait or direction.

"Don't disturb the principal. Give him his space," Sensei Malmstrom advised. He then reviewed defenses against a more insistent encounter with the principal, where the protector had to actively distract the opponent. The goal was to keep the attacker's gaze on the defender and not on the principal. When there were multiple attackers, we were instructed to line them up one in front of the other to deal with them one at a time, not all at once. At the same time, we had to maintain awareness of the person we were protecting.

While my white blood cell count remained above the neutropenic level, by the month of December I had become anemic (with a low red blood cell count). At acupuncture I mentioned to Sandy that as a result of the anemia, I had to rest a little bit more between sets of repetitions at the gym. We laughed in gratitude at the minor complaint. I'm sure the fact that I continued to work out helped me use the hemoglobin I did have in my blood more efficiently. Sandy treated points for building blood and supporting my immunity. Whatever the nature of this acupuncture magic, it was working!

At work, I felt I could resonate greater empathy with my patients. When relaying positive (malignant) biopsy results to my patients, I could describe in detail the choices and treatments to follow. In some cases, I would share my own personal experience, to help illuminate the road ahead and assure them it wasn't so bad. God has put me on this earth to do what I'm doing.

Michael needed to have his impacted wisdom teeth removed. We had decided that the best time for him would be during winter break of his junior year. That way he would be healed in time for his next major performance, the All-State Orchestra in February.

The procedure was scheduled for Thursday, December 21. We were prepared for several days of R & R with a bunch of videotapes, ice cream, and a six-pack of Ensure to sustain him. Michael took a premedication of valium the night before and slept well. The morning of the procedure, we brought his portable CD player, headphones, and an ATB techno music CD that he thought would be appropriate to listen to during his light anesthesia with nitrous oxide and local.

I read my *Radiology* journal and ladies magazines in the waiting room. After a few minutes, I thought I heard Michael laughing. About an hour later, he emerged from the suite steadier on his feet than I recall Rachel being after her wisdom teeth extraction, although we still went directly to the car. He recalled that during the procedure, he heard the doctor say that two of the four wisdom teeth had been removed, and for some reason, he found that hilarious. No wonder they call it laughing gas!

I took Michael home and positioned him comfortably on the couch. We then had a relaxing afternoon watching three videotapes, although I remember more of them than he does because of the pain medication he had taken. It was good to be thinking of someone else's health concerns rather than my own. I was so thankful to feel well enough to care for my son in time of need. As a mother, that was my primary concern.

Michael recovered quickly, without much discomfort or swelling. We enjoyed an easy few days of healing, daytime television, and videos. He was able to play a little bit of piano, although the French horn would have to wait for one to two weeks of recovery.

I had begun crocheting an Afghan in deep red chenille wool. I referred to it as a cat magnet, because every time I took it out one of our two cats would jump on it and start purring. By the third day, Michael was eating soft foods and ready to drop in on a party at one of his friend's homes.

He encouraged me to document my own treatment experiences. As there was time with my being at home, I used it to catch up on journaling my thoughts, some of which I share here.

My entry for 12/22/00: I'm, as Bernie Siegel calls it, an exceptional cancer patient. Dr. Minford gives me an A+. Chemo means being bald and getting enough sleep. The GI tract has held up, counts remain pretty good (although my hematocrit which reflects the red blood cell count isn't what it used to be, it's not bad either). Thanks to acupuncture, Zoloft, Zantac, and the support of everybody—techs at work, docs, family, friends. Jessie has been full of positive support and advice. I'm wearing the cherub earrings she gave me right now. Chemo has gotten rid of everything unnecessary: first and foremost, any cancer cells that dare remain; unwanted hair (shaving legs with less frequency); unnecessary commitments (who needs all those mall and party crowds, anyway?). You can eat tons on this catabolic medication, great this time of year. Six months from now, chemo and radiation therapy will be over, hopefully.

This is something that happens—you face it and deal with it. Breast cancer is so prevalent, it's almost like one of the natural stages of life: childhood, puberty with the onset of menses, marriage, childbearing, breast cancer, menopause (or, for some, menopause and breast cancer). As my mother is fond of pointing out, everything has its reason.

"If you stay calm in muddy water, you will understand that the mud sinks to the bottom and the water becomes clear. This is *injutsu*."—Masaaki Hatsumi[1]

Reference:

1. Hatsumi, Masaaki. *Ninpo: Wisdom for Life*. Kihon Press, 2002, p.169.

10

Happy New Year

"We'll be defending against grabs," said Mr. Elrod. "First against one and then against two attackers. I want you to stay relaxed. Drop your body weight to get out of the grab. No need to strike your partner: for this drill all I want you to do is get out by turning into the weakest part of the grab. It's like trying to hold onto a greased pig, you just can't do it. The important thing is to keep moving."

It works so well, even against the larger men in the class. A surprisingly simple, yet elegant, technique.

"Two things I learned from the Grandmaster, Hatsumi Sensei," Mr. Elrod continued, "you need to constantly off-balance your opponents to keep them problem-solving and you need to keep moving."

When Debbie, Peter, and Rebecca Powell arrived, I was working out on the Nordic Track. It was the day before cycle 3 of Cytoxan/Adriamycin, and I wanted to be sure to get my exercise in, as I wouldn't feel much like it for a couple of days afterwards. Debbie was amazed to see me exercising, but I reassured her that it actually helped keep my energy level up. After my twenty minutes on the machine, though, I'd had enough.

They were delighted to see me looking so well.

"Thankfully," I told them, "I don't feel particularly bad, I just get tired by 9:00 at night. I've felt worse when I've had the flu." The Powells usually came to visit us for a few days after their Christmas holiday visit to Peter's family in West Virginia. This year being a little unusual, they just spent one night.

The next morning, I had my usual pre-chemo breakfast of oatmeal and a cup of green tea.

"You have to smile when you say the words green tea because of all the e's," I told Rebecca. Rebecca tasted some and proclaimed it not too bad. Debbie accompanied me to my chemotherapy session, while Peter and Rebecca explored the mall, particularly, the Build-a-Bear store.

Like AJ, Debbie was somber as we were driving to the outpatient oncology department, but I reassured her it wouldn't be bad at all. I introduced Debbie to the receptionist, Terry, and to the oncology nurses, Patty and Colleen.

"My best friend came all the way from New Hampshire to be with me," I beamed.

"What a true friend," Colleen commented as she took us back. I selected a cozy corner chair, and Deb took a seat beside me. As the December air was chilly, it took a warm compress to induce my veins to emerge, but Colleen, bless her hands, started the IV with no problem.

As the premedications ran in, I described to Deb how they made me feel a little "spacey" and tired. The whole process was totally new to Debbie, a psychologist, and she was interested in hearing about every step.

"Thanks to chemo, menopause in 6 weeks," I confided to Debbie; "it sure beats years of perimenopausal symptoms and takes the guesswork out of when it's going to happen."

"You look on the bright side of everything," laughed Deb. I explained what Colleen was doing when she brought over the syringe of Adriamycin.

"Look at this," I told Deb, "it's red! Colleen has to put it in slowly, diluting it with a salt solution, so it doesn't harm my vein." I mentioned that some people required indwelling IV's (ports) for chemotherapy, if they didn't have large enough peripheral veins.

We talked about more than chemotherapy, though. Friends since the age of ten, we're like sisters and have so much to share. We were grateful to have this couple of hours to catch up with each other, although the setting was not our customary bookstore or cafe. We're blessed with a friendship that endures through thick and thin, and we noted that this was one of those thinner times.

Debbie drove us home, and I planted myself as a couch potato. In a few minutes, Peter and Rebecca arrived with the newly created bear, a cute curly-haired light brown teddy in red shorts. They left all too soon for a day exploring Washington, D.C.

Michael was home with me. I took a nap, serenaded by his beautiful piano practicing. He was working on a Chopin Fantaisie that I particularly loved.

The following day at acupuncture, Sandy worked on supporting my energy, as my level of fatigue was slightly greater.

"It's all about balance and movement. If the energy (Qi) keeps moving, the body will heal itself," she told me. At the end of the session, Sandy needled a point in each hand called Small Intestine 3, to touch my wood and fire. In Chinese medicine the five elements, wood, fire, metal, water, and earth are fundamental to understanding the balance and flow of Qi within nature. In his book *Acupuncture: Energy Balancing for Body, Mind & Spirit*, Peter Mole says:

"Each element represents a different quality in the human being, just as each season brings a different quality to the entire natural world."[1]

Sunday was New Year's Eve. Michael had sufficiently recovered from his wisdom teeth surgery to enjoy a friend's party. AJ and I thought this would be a good New Year's Eve to spend quietly at home.

We spoke to our families. Even Rachel called from Israel. Popping the cork on a bottle of sparkling apple cider (no alcohol on chemo), we watched on TV as the Times Square ball dropped. A toast to a healthy and happy New Year, one better than the last. Like the image of a baby symbolizing the New Year, I had no hair. To me, it represented a fresh start and some hard-won wisdom.

References:

1. Mole, Peter. *Acupuncture: Energy Balancing for Body, Mind, & Spirit*. Element Books, Inc. Boston, MA 1992, p.27.

11

Halftime

Defenses from the ground are difficult, but important to learn. Of course, it's preferable to avoid being pinned on the ground, but fights may wind up that way and one must learn what to do. Pinned on your back with your arms up: lift up your hips and throw your opponent off with all of your body weight. Then, pin your opponent, best with his face down, so that it is difficult for him to kick or punch you.

Defenses against being pinned on your stomach are more difficult. If one of your arms is beneath you, or if your knee is bent, you have some leeway to move and throw your opponent off.

"Don't stop moving until your attacker stops moving," says Mrs. Elrod. "If it's a choice between you or your attacker going home, it will be you. Fighting is about ATTITUDE."

January, 2001, a new year in a new millennium. Rachel returned safely to New Haven. Michael's winter break was over. At work, I was filled with a sense of calling, the "this is what I was meant to do" feeling. I knew I was put here on this earth to read mammos and counsel women about breast disease. All I was going through could benefit womankind.

I conserved my energy, going to bed by 9 or 10 at night. Working only three days a week was certainly helpful. One who likes a routine, I continued my exercising on the Nordic track or at the gym, as well as attending karate classes.

Then there was the feisty part of me that wanted to do what I wasn't supposed to do.

"I want to stay up late, drink alcohol, and brawl," I pronounced to AJ one day. Not like I ever did any of those things before, and not like I was really going to go out and do them when I was able to. They epitomized all I wasn't supposed to do, so I wanted to. Just like a child you say no to, don't creates do:

"Don't think of an elephant." So, what's on your mind now? Is it a cute one like Dumbo or one of those big ones you see in the circus?

One afternoon while I was home, I received a call from our rabbi, Susan Grossman. It was so thoughtful. She'd heard about my chemotherapy treatment and was calling to see how I was doing. She had lost her own mother to metastatic breast cancer.

"Thank God, I'm feeling well," I told her. "Having no hair teaches you a lot about vanity," I continued. We talked about Orthodox women who shave their heads. I told her that I would be happy to advise anyone in the congregation going through a similar experience. The Rabbi said if I needed anything I should give her a call. I was on the prayer list for the temple. Prayer works. I knew I was in Good Hands.

"May God who blessed our ancestors, Abraham, Isaac, and Jacob, Sarah, Rebecca, Rachel, and Leah, bring blessing and healing to Sinda Bat Shmuel (my Hebrew name, used in prayer). May the Holy One mercifully restore her to health and vigor, granting her physical and spiritual well-being, together with all others who are ill. And although Shabbat is a time to refrain from petitions, we yet hope and pray that healing is at hand. And let us say: Amen."[1]

One of my workdays, I was assigned to a busy imaging center near a hospital. It was a day of nonstop cases and consultations. In the early afternoon, I was called over to CT scan. The technologist was having difficulty starting an IV on a chemotherapy patient with poor veins. I greeted the patient, who was pale and wearing a turban with a delicate floral pattern. After placing the tourniquet around her arm, I scanned it for a suitable vein. Her skin was hairless and smooth, like my own, due to the chemotherapy. I started the IV. As the fluid flowed into her vein, I thought I felt the warmth and slight buzz I associated with receiving my IV chemotherapy treatment. But no, this time I was the doctor and not the patient.

January 19, 2001: a day of mini-celebration. It was the day I completed my fourth cycle of chemotherapy. I was halfway through and all done with the "big guns" Cytoxan and Adriamycin! Farewell to the IV bag of Cytoxan and the big red syringe of Adria. Never give up! Never give in!

Sandie was there with me. This time she had come with a big tackle box full of jewelry-making paraphernalia. She proceeded to make me earrings and a necklace of matching jade-colored fused glass, as we sat there and chatted. "Chemo entertainment by Sandie," we joked. Everyone should be so lucky!

To my amazement, as I reported to Sandy Johnson at acupuncture the following day, I still felt like a regular, healthy person. My last bout of the flu had been worse than anything I'd experienced thus far. Sandy continued treatment directed to supporting me through the chemotherapy. CV12: Alarm point of the stomach. Whatever the points were, they were working, and I was grateful for that.

We discussed the network of loving people one discovers when going through something like cancer treatment. So many have had breast cancer or have been touched by the disease in a loved one. The peaceful surroundings of the acupuncture suite were conducive to relaxation and visualization. As I lay there during treatment, my mind wandered. I imagined myself supported on a hammock of woven golden thread held up by Sandy Johnson, Julie Elrod, my friends and family. Sandy Johnson: acupuncture, positive imagery. Mrs. Elrod: fighting spirit. Leslie, Wayne, AJ and the children: supporting family. Deb, Jessie, Sandie: inspiring, positive friends, love of career and community.

I did feel tired through the weekend and on the Monday after the chemotherapy. I was heartened by a card I received in the mail from my brother, Wayne. There was a cute bear on the outside of the card. On the inside was Wayne's encouraging message:

"Bear with it, you're halfway there!" My stomach felt a little unsettled, but the "Whopper" on Tuesday helped quite a bit. What an unusual craving. Nowhere anecdotally or in the medical literature have I heard of anyone enjoying Whoppers so much during chemotherapy.

I actually napped a little in the afternoon. I invited all the animals up on the bed with me. My dog Meg O'Bite appreciated the special treat and had a guilty angle to her ears while we napped. The cats felt a sense of entitlement to the master bed. As Jennifer (Jessie's daughter) viewed it, I was surrounded by angels looking after me.

Just as I was feeling down and out, the phone rang. Debbie! How does she always know to call at the right time to lift my sagging spirits? Such are the mysterious ways of friendship.

Back at work at the mammo center to a busy day: several biopsies, many mammograms to read. Then, on the way home, a stop at the lab for my weekly visit to check my counts. Michael's piano students had cancelled due to illness, so we decided to rush and dress to make it to the 6:10 karate class. A great and inspiring class, as always.

At the end of the class, Mrs. Elrod had everyone sit along the edge of the mat. I thought that someone was going to be testing for a stripe or next belt level. Then she began to speak about an award for a student with perseverance through difficult times.

"How neat, I wonder who's going to get that?" I thought. As Mrs. Elrod continued, I heard her say my name. I was awarded the Student of the Year for the dojo. Perseverance, when there was literally a sword to my heart.

Mr. Elrod presented me with a real Japanese sword. I couldn't believe it.

"Is this for me?" I asked incredulously.

"Yes, of course," he smiled. After class, everyone clustered around congratulating me, some of them asking to see the sharp blade. We called Rachel when we were back home. She was so proud of her Mama!

AJ's 50th birthday was coming up on Saturday, the 27th. His father Papa Bob's 80th birthday was one week later, and a big celebration was being planned in New Jersey for both of them. People would be coming from all over the country to celebrate. There would be as many people as candles on Papa's cake!

I wanted to get AJ a special gift for his 50th birthday. He never asks for anything, but he did mention that he liked the black leather jacket one of his acquaintances was wearing. That was all the hint I needed. I headed over to the leather store in the mall and picked out a zip-up style leather jacket with a removable Thinsulate lining that I knew would look good on him. I liked it so much that I tried on a women's leather jacket with a similar lining. It would be good for three seasons in this climate. I'd always wanted a leather jacket, and it fit me perfectly. Ah well, a little gift to myself to celebrate the halfway point of chemotherapy. Retail Therapy soothes again.

The afternoon of AJ's birthday, we went to the gym. I wore a scarf over my head, since Doris would be a little too hot to exercise in. I only wished I could have been like those men who shave their heads and go around the gym bald, feeling cool and macho. A bald lady would attract undue attention, though. What a double standard.

I felt strong, although my heart was beating quickly, and I needed to rest quite a bit between the sets of weight repetitions. A little more hemoglobin would help. All was fine until I got to the stairclimber. I selected my favorite machine, with a view outside a window. As usual, I grabbed a nearby ladies magazine to pass the time while exercising. My typical workout was 20 minutes on the machine.

I did fine until about 16 minutes into it, when I was more out of breath than usual. I plodded away, for another minute or so. By about 18 minutes, I realized that if I continued anymore I would faint. Since I was exercising for my health and not to make myself sick, I immediately stepped off the machine and sat down on the floor nearby. So much for trying not to be obvious. Nobody seemed to take notice of me, fortunately. I got up as soon as I could walk over to the chairs in the lounge, recovering after sitting there for several minutes. I guess this anemia thing really was taking its toll.

That evening, we had AJ's birthday celebration. I made his favorite standing rib roast, and we had a fancy hazelnut cream cake from the mall. Rachel called just as we were getting to the presents. It's as if she were there with us. We were all looking forward to seeing her in New Jersey at Papa's celebration the following weekend.

AJ's birthday was usually Super Bowl weekend, and 2001 was no exception. Sunday we ate subs and watched the game and, of course, the commercials. This year was particularly exciting because our own Baltimore Ravens were in it, and they won! The parade downtown was two days later, on a cold, rainy Tuesday morning. I was otherwise occupied, and the cold, not to mention the crowds, was not the environment for one on chemo.

There were a couple of itchy spots on my side. One of my dermatologist colleagues worked me into his schedule. It was shingles. Shingles? I was lucky to feel itchy rather than pain! He prescribed me an antiviral medication, Famvir, to shorten the course and severity of the ailment.

Later that day, I thought to myself:

"To heck with this chemo stuff, I'm going to the gym." I took things slowly, resting between sets, lowering the settings on the Stairclimber. This time I made it through without feeling faint. The workout was energizing and a salve to my spirit.

At work in the second half of the week I paced myself. I was glad I wasn't a surgeon on her feet all day. The ongoing support of my staff and coworkers kept me going. Our receptionist Sandra, who had seen her son through cancer treatment, was encouraging, telling me how well I looked. Angie our health assistant brought me homemade cakes and other treats to sustain me. Thursday after work I stopped by at the lab for the weekly counts.

Michael and I attended our karate class. That evening a photographer was there, taking posed pictures of those who had signed up. Michael didn't want one of himself, since he'd had one done fairly recently. I would have normally declined the opportunity as well, but I wanted a picture of myself at this particular time. I wore a black stocking cap on my head during the karate classes, as I didn't want Doris leaping across the room. The children had given me a set of dreadlock-type hairpieces, which I pinned to the inside of the cap to look like curls coming down the sides. They said it made me look cool.

I posed for the pictures in my cap and black gi, holding a sword. With the photographer's digital equipment, I was able to view them immediately. I selected a serious pose, one where I looked like I really meant business. Take that, chemo!

The following day I worked at the mammography center. Around 9:30 in the morning I received a call from the oncology nurse Colleen. I thought it was so nice of her to call and see how I was. A few minutes into the conversation, I realized she was calling for a reason. My blood count had come back: I was even more anemic, with a hematocrit of 29.8. I had also become neutropenic, with a total white blood cell count of 1400 and only 600 neutrophils. That meant I was at increased risk for infection.

She told me I needed to start taking the Tequin, a strong antibiotic, to guard against bacterial infections. I mentioned that I had developed a sore spot on the inside of my cheek, which hurt when I swallowed. I thought it might be candidiasis, a yeast infection that occurs in immune suppressed people. Colleen agreed that I should start taking the antifungal medication, Diflucan.

"I guess I should cancel the trip to my father-in-law's 80th birthday party in New Jersey this weekend," I said.

"That would be a good idea," replied Colleen. I then phoned AJ to let him know. At first he suggested that he stay home with me, but I was insistent that he and Michael go to the celebration.

"It's a celebration for both you and your father! I won't keep you from that. Besides, I feel fine," I reassured him, "I just need to be away from crowds of people." The rest of the day, I was apprehensive about exposure to people around me. Fortunately, I was only working with a handful of technologists, none of whom were contagious for anything. I was scheduled to work the following Monday, but I called our physician scheduler Vicki and told her it would be better for me to be off that day due to my low counts. She reassured me that she would take care of the schedule and hoped I would be feeling better.

Everybody left for the weekend. I stayed at home in relative isolation due to the neutropenia. I left the house only to walk my dog Meg and to go to my Saturday acupuncture session. Using points on my back, Sandy directed the treatment toward building my blood counts and immunity,.

At acupuncture as well as at home I worked on visualizing my bone marrow cranking up. Production was under the supervision of the good witch Glenda from *The Wizard of Oz*. She created new white blood cells and reticulocytes (red blood cell precursors) with her magic wand. The brand new white cells sparkled on the assembly line. They gleamed with health, vitality and strength to fight unwanted microbes. I imagined the reticulocytes as a volleyball team, like Rachel's winning high school team, dancing around, warming up, ready to jump into the bloodstream as powerful red blood cells. My imagery then shifted to paratroopers being launched from a helicopter into battle. Those red cells were rarin' to go, armed with their weapons of oxygen-carrying hemoglobin for all of my body's cells. As a physician, particularly a radiologist who deals with the visual, my imagery took on physiologic details others would not necessarily envision.

I was determined to make the best of it, to enjoy the solitude and rest. I wanted to do something constructive. Listening to lively, upbeat music, I worked on the afghan I was crocheting. The soft, chenille wool drew my two cats Gracie and Micetro to it. They couldn't resist kneading and laying on it. The only problem was flipping over my work to start a new row, dislodging whomever had been in the coveted position for the moment. Meg guarded me from intruders. Between my guard dog and the antifungal, antibacterial, and antiviral medications I was on, nothing could get me!

Late Saturday afternoon AJ and the children called from New Jersey. Everyone at the party missed me and sent their best for my return to good health. I was gladdened by the warm wishes, although I felt fine and in good health—except for some itchy, mildly painful shingles lesions and a little mouth sore...well, maybe I wasn't totally fine.

The mouth sore persisted, despite my baking soda rinses and antifungal medication. Dr. Minford checked it on Tuesday. He thought I should discontinue the Diflucan and Tequin and switch to Penicillin. We delayed my starting Taxol for several days, from Friday to the following Tuesday, to give my counts a chance to recuperate. The Tuesday schedule for Taxol would actually be better, as the myalgias, which commonly followed, set in on day 3 of the cycle, and I could schedule the Friday off.

It was with apprehension that I awaited the results of my next blood count that week. If I remained neutropenic, the Taxol could be delayed further and I would need Neupogen (Granulocyte Colony Stimulating Factor), a medication used to enhance white blood cell production. If my hematocrit remained below 30, I would require treatment with Procrit (recombinant human erythropoietin) to increase red cell production. I was thankful such medications existed to boost the marrow of chemotherapy patients. Certainly my father didn't have the benefits of those in 1960.

This time, however, Colleen called me with good news. My white count was 830, out of the neutropenic range. In addition, my hematocrit had jumped from 29.8 to 32.9. I'm convinced it was the acupuncture boosted by my visualizations that stimulated my bone marrow into action. Now all systems were go for the next phase: Taxol.

"When you get into a tight place and everything goes against you, till it seems as though you could not hang on a minute longer, never give up then, for that is just the place and time that the tide will turn."-Harriet Beecher Stowe.

References:

1. The Rabbinical Assembly: the United Synagogue of Conservative Judaism. *Siddur Sim Shalom for Shabbat and Festivals.* The Rabbinical Assembly, 1998, p.144.

12

Here's Looking at Yew

In martial arts as in anything it is important to learn to deal with fear and an adrenalin surge: to be able to act instead of freeze. We have done several drills in class to hone this skill. In one such drill, we were in groups of three with one person in the center with his eyes closed. One of the two others would yell and attack or one would yell and the other would attack. As soon as she hears the yell, the one in the center opens her eyes and defends. The defender needs to overcome any sensation of freezing in fright in order to react quickly.

I was working with two other women. In the center with my eyes closed, arms up and knees slightly bent in a defensive posture, I suddenly heard a loud man's yell! I opened my eyes to find Mr. Elrod beside me and one of my female partners attacking. Talk about surprise!

"I thought somebody had a sex change there for a second," I laughed. Later in class, we all stood around the edge of the large mat, facing out, with our eyes closed. The lights in the dojo were turned off, and someone at an unknown time would grab us from behind. Opening our eyes, we had to yell and defend. I prided myself on my loud yells—it must have been those first ten years in Queens, N.Y. that taught me to give a good holler.

It was the Monday before my Taxol was to begin. I felt more energetic at the gym, with my hematocrit up by about 10% from my previous foray there. I wore a bandana on my head, like those big muscular guys. I felt sure that I looked cool like they did, not like a lady on chemotherapy. I ran into someone from our temple and chatted with him about our workouts and kids. No way anyone could tell I was on chemo, so I thought. A few days later, though, I received a wonderful letter in the mail from him, with two scarves included. He had worn them himself during races to benefit kids with cancer. He could see I was on chemotherapy, and prayed that I continued to feel so well.

Taxol (also known as paclitaxel) and Taxotere (docetaxel) are in the relatively new category of chemotherapy agents called taxanes. Taxanes were originally derived from the bark and needles of the yew tree.[1] Knowing that piece of trivia, I wondered about the first brave soul who tried it for medicinal purposes.

Taxol is dissolved in a highly allergenic camphor-based solution. As a result, it requires quite a bit of premedication, that needs to be taken on schedule. I took 20 mg. of the steroid dexamethasone twelve and six hours before the Taxol. That meant setting my alarm clock for 5 a.m., so I would have the second dose six hours before my 11 a.m. appointment. I awoke that morning with my face bright red from the high dose of steroid, and my eyes were puffy from the fluid I retained. Another side effect: I had tons of energy, but I paced myself so as not to overdo it.

When I settled into an armchair in the chemotherapy suite, I noticed I was next to one of my patients I had recently done an ultrasound on. Fortunately, due to the context and, perhaps my cap instead of Doris, she didn't recognize me. I like to keep my doctor and patient roles separate.

Sandie arrived, holding purple tulips for me. I'd never seen purple tulips. They were gorgeous! We put them by the window, where we and other patients could admire them.

I asked the nurse Colleen about whether I would notice any hair growing back yet on the Taxol. She did say that some patients get downy growth while they're on it. Before the Taxol, I received more IV premedications: Benadryl, which gave me a "buzz," Cimetidine, another dose of Dexamethasone, as well as the antinausea drug Anzemet. With that regimen, my immune system could handle any allergen! Colleen started the Taxol dripping in at a slow rate at first. As I felt fine, she was able to advance the rate somewhat. After about an hour, Dr. Minford came by, to see how I was doing.

"I'm fine," I said. "So when do you think I can start sparring?" I bet he'd never heard that one from someone with an IV dripping chemo into her arm.

"Not until you're done with chemotherapy," he replied with a grin. Oh well, then I wouldn't have to worry about a cap staying on. By the time AJ picked me up, it was about 3:30p.m. Colleen apologized for keeping me so long, but I reassured her I didn't have anything else on my schedule for the day.

I woke up the next morning for work still quite red in the face, an appropriate color for Valentine's Day. I maintained an increased energy level from the steroids, quite a difference from the day after a Cytoxan/Adriamycin treatment.

Years of training, dedication, and now my own personal experience with the object of mammography's search have taught me that reading mammograms is a sacred task that has been entrusted to me. My work puts me face to face with breast cancer on a daily basis. This day was no different. I spoke to a patient with a suspicious-looking mass detected by a mammogram and ultrasound, informing her that she needed a biopsy. She was stricken with a look of panic upon hearing the word biopsy.

"This is just why we do mammography," I continued, "to find things so small they can't be felt, when they're curable with the least amount of surgery."

I went on to explain that she could have either an ultrasound-guided incisional core biopsy or a preoperative needle localization and excisional biopsy. I then gave her the English translation for those terms, sharing that I'd been through both of them and they weren't bad. The worst part was the anxiety waiting for the results. We scheduled her ultrasound-guided biopsy for three days later to minimize the number of sleepless nights, as I knew all too well. There's just too much breast cancer around. I want to see a time when it's not a daily event in my mammography practice.

I had arranged to be off on Friday to drive Michael to his All-State Band weekend in Baltimore. In the morning I noticed the onset of myalgias and took two Aleve, as Colleen had suggested. The myalgias weren't too bad, though. They just felt like random pains periodically occurring in different muscles all over my body, no worse than the muscle soreness I had experienced the day after a hard sparring workout in karate. I dropped Michael off around noon. We arranged to meet after his concert on Sunday.

I saw Gordon, my psychiatrist, later in the day. We talked about the halfway point of my chemotherapy, followed by my nadir and missing the birthday celebration in New Jersey. I was sanguine about it and grateful that my counts had improved and the shingles and mouth sore had resolved. At least I had a crocheted afghan to show for it. The Taxol wasn't too bad yet, and I was hopeful about getting some hair out of it. So far, nothing had been too bad. I felt like I had been in a velvet parachute protecting me through the whole thing.

Acupuncture the next day was well timed, as I was still experiencing myalgias. Sandy needled points relating to the muscles and tendons. I focused on my visualization during the session. I've heard and read others describing their battle with cancer, the war on cancer, and images of cells fighting cancer. Although I study martial arts, images of war do not resonate with me. The visualizations I come up with reflect my daily life and concerns, but I can relate to them. I returned to my mundane laundry imagery: Cytoxan/Adriamycin was the wash cycle, cleansing my body of any stray cancer cells. Taxol served as the rinse cycle. Radiation therapy would be the dryer. Whether the images were logical or not, I wanted to use every image, every fiber of my being to come through this experience alive and healthy.

As I looked out at the bare trees, my thoughts again wandered to the seasons. My diagnosis came in October, Breast Cancer Awareness month; surgery and chemotherapy in the autumn. I lost my hair as the trees lost their leaves (at least my hair didn't turn all sorts of colors first). Now in the winter, I had entered menopause, the "chemical" menopause that results from chemotherapy. With spring will come the end of chemotherapy; warmth, sunshine, and radiant radiation; new leaves and new hair.

Later in the day AJ and I went to the movies. We saw "Crouching Tiger, Hidden Dragon," the beautifully done martial arts film directed by Ange Lee. I loved the fact that there were so many women martial artists in it. I chose to identify with the more experienced woman warrior, Shu Lien, although bald as I was without Doris, I looked more like Master Li. Baldness conveys the look of spiritual wisdom. Such wisdom doesn't come easily, as I was learning.

Now that I'd begun Taxol, though, I was ready for hair. I started doing a daily follicle check. On Sunday morning, I thought I could see a new follicle. While food shopping, I anxiously purchased a magazine of short hairstyles. By the time it was my turn on the checkout line, I had picked out my new 'do.

That afternoon, we drove to Baltimore for the All-State concert. I hadn't been around so many people since the nadir of my chemotherapy, though, so I tried to stay away from being densely surrounded by the crowd. It's amazing how, after only two and a half days of practice together, those groups sounded so wonderful. We heard the orchestra first, followed by the chorus. Michael was in the band, which was the last group to perform:

Trauermusik, WWV73..Richard Wagner
Children's March: "Over the Hills and Far Away"..........Percy Grainger
Festive Overture, Opus 96..............................Dmitri Shostakovich

"Listening to the music inside our soul slowly and decisively allows the plan to unfold and our destiny will be transcribed onto our soul. The journey of purpose is charted as we open ourselves to the possibilities of another path."—Diane Anselmo.[2]

References:

1. Love, SM. *Dr. Susan Love's Breast Book.* Perseus Publishing, 2000, p.383.

2. Anselmo, Diane. *Women's Choices, Women's Lives: Learn from 30 Not So Ordinary Women How the Power of Choice Can Change Your Life.* IUniverse, Inc. Lincoln, NE 2002, p.87.

13

From Winter to Spring

In karate we did a warm-up drill of rolls around the mat. Forward rolls, one right after another. A little dizzying and tiring for me, but I just took it slowly and steadily. The challenging part was to keep the cap on my head. At one point it did fall off, revealing my bald head. I just picked up the cap, stuck it back on my head, and kept rolling. One of my adult classmates Susan later commented that I looked really tough without my hat. Cancer and martial arts are not for the faint of heart.

After class Gail, another student and a fellow physician, showed us her gold "Nin" 忍 pendant that had been crafted by a jeweler friend of hers. It could be made in either gold or silver. Several of us ordered them. They would be ready in about six weeks. I thought it would be a fitting commemoration of my perseverance through and completion of chemotherapy.

On Thursday, February 28, Michael's French horn teacher Karen drove him up to Pittsburgh for his All-Eastern Orchestra rehearsal weekend. AJ and I left on Saturday, a bright crisp day. It was the beginning of Rachel's Spring break, and she was excited to be joining us. We picked her up at the Pittsburgh airport. I had reserved a two-bedroom suite for us at a hotel. It was my first time out of town since October, and I was determined to do it right! When we checked into our room, I proudly showed Rachel the new down on my head. She agreed that it was definitely coming in. Maybe no wig by my birthday [June 1]?

The next day was cold and blustery. We had to wait outside in a crowd before the auditorium doors were opened for the concert. I began to get nervous in the crowd: I was still taking chemotherapy and did not need the exposure to all of these people. I was beginning to reach the point of telling one of the officials that I was a chemotherapy patient and had to be let in out of the crowd immediately when the doors were opened and we were allowed in.

My anxiety quickly dissipated as we sank into the comfortable seats of the Heinz auditorium. There was a velvet curtain on the stage. The orchestra was a large ensemble of 120 members. These were the best high school musicians on the East Coast. What a beautiful rich sound they created. It was hard to believe that they'd rehearsed together for only three days.

After the concert, we ate dinner before setting out for home. Michael told us about the other musicians he'd met. He had known some of them from previous music programs he'd participated in. Several were high school seniors hoping to attend music conservatories the following year.

It was snowing when we started our ride home. AJ drove our all-wheel drive sedan, which did well in these conditions. Within the first hour of the trip, the snowstorm picked up. We proceeded slowly, following the taillights of cars ahead of us, since the lane markers were obscured by a layer of snow. Several cars skidded off the road. Rachel and I were at the edge of our seats, each of us in turn warning AJ when he was out of the lane. The car brakes labored slowly in the snow, and we hoped we wouldn't have to use them on short notice. It took us seven and a half hours to make the trip that had taken us only four hours the day before. Our prayers had been answered: we were home safe and sound.

AJ and Rachel had to leave early the next morning for an analytical chemistry trade show in New Orleans. Rachel helped staff AJ's company booth at the exhibition. She had worked in his lab over the summer and knew enough about the science and product line to be an asset in the booth. She even practiced some of the Chinese she had been studying at school on several of the foreign scientists.

Michael and I shoveled out our driveway from the storm. I was initially apprehensive about how helpful I could be, but I found that I could shovel, although more slowly than usual, resting frequently. I noticed my heart pounding, working under the strain of the exercise and the anemia. But I did it! I shoveled snow while on chemotherapy! We finished our manual labor and treated ourselves to large mugs of hot chocolate with marshmallows and whipped cream.

Tuesday was my second cycle of Taxol. Since AJ was out of town, I had arranged for Sandie to drive me. While sitting with me during the chemotherapy session, Sandie showed me the wonders of her new Palm Pilot. I was amazed at the amount of data that little thing could hold. In addition to the appointments and address book functions, it even had a program that turned the screen into a mirror. I had read about medical applications for the Palm operating system. I knew what would constitute my next Retail Therapy treatment.

In the chair next to mine was an elderly woman receiving chemotherapy. Her two daughters sat with her. Sandie and I chatted with all of them. The woman was also receiving Taxol but for bladder, not breast, cancer. I thought to myself how Taxol was cleansing my whole body of cancerous cells-breast, bladder, or any other renegade parts. The bladder surgery preceding her chemotherapy had weakened her considerably, and she was having a hard time with chemotherapy, experiencing fatigue and nausea. I described how helpful acupuncture had been for me and suggested she try it.

Acupuncture the following Saturday again coincided with the peak of my myalgias. Sandy continued to use points supporting my muscles and tendons. As it was the change of season, she also worked on shifting my bodymindspirit into Spring: a transition from the dormant to awakening, quiescence to activity, and, as I saw it, from no hair to hair!

With AJ and Rachel's return from the conference came a burst of activity. I wanted to make the most of the remaining week of Rachel's Spring break. Rachel commented that I was like a bald cheerleader with my enthusiasm. Sunday, we jogged around nearby Centennial Park, a 2½-mile stretch. I always ran faster with her than by myself and appreciated the additional motivation. Later in the afternoon, we baked Hamantaschen, triangular filled pastries traditionally eaten around the Jewish holiday of Purim this time of year.

I was off Monday, and Rachel and I went to Staples to pick up some school supplies she needed. There it was, a Palm Pilot! On sale! I just had to have it. So I bought it.

Rachel and Michael commented that my hair was thickening and growing every day. Interestingly, my eyebrows were starting to thin out. Go figure. Both of the children liked to kiss my bald head, which was like a baby's with its fine down. All the love you emanate comes flowing back to you.

I felt joyful on the first day of Spring. With Spring would come the end of chemotherapy; as the leaves regrew, so would my hair. My hematocrit was up to 12, and I noticed an increase in my energy level at the gym. I thought it miraculous that I continued to feel so well on chemotherapy.

A brochure describing chemotherapy that I happened to notice at Dr. Minford's office recommended indulging yourself during treatment. I guess I shouldn't feel too guilty about all the Retail Therapy: leather jacket, Palm Pilot, necklace, a couple of pairs of shoes, which I haven't bothered to mention on these pages. AJ commented that it's a good thing Imelda Marcos didn't have breast cancer.

Back at work, I was busy reading mammograms and doing biopsies. As a physician, I draw on experience from all of my life in my interactions with patients. My own diagnosis of breast cancer can help illuminate the path for some of them, who want to know what comes next after a positive biopsy result. Telling an elderly woman that her biopsy showed cancer cells, I shared my own experience and described the surgery that would follow. While it may not make the news any better, it does answer some questions. Yes, there is productive life after a breast cancer diagnosis.

March 27: the second to last chemotherapy treatment! I attained a greater understanding of the vagaries of patient veins through my own chemotherapy experience. Invariably, as good as my hand and forearm veins usually are, they would contract when I entered the chemotherapy suite. It must have been either the cool ambient temperature or my own anxiety, but I presented the nurse Colleen with a bit of a challenge. She, in turn, was always up to the task! I was premedicated and, thankfully, again took the Taxol like a champ. Sandie arrived a few minutes into the premedication, and regaled me for the duration of the treatment.

Michael's Spring break came in April. The Yale Symphony Orchestra was playing in Carnegie Hall on April 10. We went by way of Princeton to bring Nana and Papa to hear Rachel. The concert was at 8 p.m. We drove into New York early and met Rachel for dinner at one of the nearby restaurants. Rachel left early to join the orchestra. We finished up and made our way to Carnegie Hall.

It was painful for Papa to walk. Slowly, finally AJ eased him into his velvet seat. The Yale Symphony Orchestra performed Verdi's "Requiem" with the Yale Glee Club, Freshman Chorus, and Camerata. Watching his granddaughter play Carnegie Hall with his alma mater's orchestra, Papa listened intently, a look of contentment settling onto his face.

14

Celebration

Karate, Olympic sports, chemotherapy: 90% mental, 10% physical. So much of training is mental, seeing oneself as a warrior. This is something I've had to consciously cultivate. I wasn't brought up thinking of myself that way. Rather, I was raised in the sweet-little-girl mode.

When I'm training in karate and feel intimidated by an opponent, such as one who has spent years studying other martial arts as well as ninjutsu, I've noticed he can get the better of me more easily. But I'm learning. I'm learning to keep coming back, watching what my opponents do so I can learn their tricks. Dr. Gene's throat grab works nicely to control attackers; Mr. John, although tall and lanky, bends his knees and keeps his body weight so low that he's difficult to throw.

I'll take a hit to the jaw and learn the hard way to get out of the way of a punch. What makes a winner is not never being defeated, but keeping at it after facing setbacks. Winning takes discipline, like anything else; discipline, as required in studying medicine or playing the piano. Perseverance, diligence, and practice. I will prevail. I will keep training my mind as well as my body to cultivate the fortitude I need to endure. I cannot afford to think otherwise. This is my life: I must survive.

"A correct heart will protect your mind and body."—Bud Malmstrom.[1]

It was a mild April Sunday afternoon when I picked up Sandie at her house. We drove to nearby Glen Burnie for a Pampered Chef Bingo get together, sponsored in part by Norine McKenzie. Norine had worked with us as a receptionist and health assistant in our former Radiology Department. Now she was one of the referral coordinators in Family Practice. The numerous referrals I needed lately got us back in touch.

Norine had arranged a reunion for us, inviting several of the technologists from our old department. Sandie and I walked into the reception hall filled with long rows of tables. I spotted our previous ultrasound techs Sheryle and Carol and went running over to them. They had heard about my recent diagnosis.

"Stacey, you look great!" beamed Sheryle as we hugged.

"Thanks! How do you like Doris?" I replied. Sheryle gave me a quizzical look.

"Doris, my wig—I named her," I explained. We laughed and grabbed some refreshments as we caught up on the past few months.

Soon it was time for Bingo, with prizes from the Pampered Chef catalogue. I hadn't played Bingo since I was 8 years old in a Catskills resort, and we had just as much fun. The suspense of the turning cage filled with numbers, filling in our cards, and…almost winning. It was the company and the hilarity that made the afternoon.

April 17, 2001: my last chemotherapy treatment, oh long-awaited day! I brought in my favorite: a Red Velvet cake. AJ picked up a couple of pizzas for all of us before going off to work. Sandie arrived with a balloon bouquet for me, as well as a personally crafted certificate of congratulations.

There I was, last Taxol dripping in and munching on pizza. Not exactly your typical image of chemotherapy. One of my recent CT patients was there getting chemotherapy. She recognized me and greeted me cheerfully, wishing me well. She was about my age and had also remained active while in treatment.

As Michael had expressed curiosity about the place where I received chemotherapy, I told him he could pick me up. He came by after school and shared in the pizza and cake. My IV was removed, and I was done. Finished with chemotherapy. It was over! Hair is on the way!

Once the euphoria of the steroids and last day of chemotherapy wore off, it was back to work again, back to the daily encounter with breast cancer in its various guises. I performed a mammogram and ultrasound on a patient with a suspicious lump in her breast. She had tears in her eyes as I examined her and scanned the mass with the ultrasound probe. She suspected the worst. Her mother had died after a long battle with breast cancer, having undergone chemotherapy, which had sickened and weakened her.

"Chemotherapy is improving all the time," I said hopefully. "I just finished it yesterday!" The patient looked at me in disbelief. It wasn't exactly what she was expecting to hear from one of her doctors. I then proceeded to explain that she needed a breast biopsy of the lump, possibly by ultrasound guidance. It wasn't all that painful, since it's done with local anesthetic. She was grateful to me for sharing my experience and left my office perhaps a little more at ease with what the future would hold.

That evening after work, I went over to Sandie's house to watch my brother Wayne on "Emeril." The show had been prerecorded in New York on Valentine's Day. Emeril entered the set amidst much excitement and enthusiastic applause. He walked right up to my brother as if he were a long lost friend and greeted him with a warm hug! Sandie and I made homemade brownies topped with ice cream, as BAM! Emeril kicked up avocados a notch.

Thursday and Friday were long, busy work days. I arrived home from work Friday evening tired, feeling my last bout of Taxol myalgias. I plopped down in the chair in my bedroom, drained. The phone rang and it was Deb. She had called to congratulate me on the completion of chemotherapy. Tired as I was, I expressed apprehension about my being able to go to the beach house in Martha's Vineyard we rented with two other couples during a week in July.

"I don't know how I'll feel after radiation if I'm so tired now," I said. "I might not want to do much. What fun will I be if I need to rest?"

"So we'll rest together," Debbie reassured me.

AJ, Michael and I drove up to New Jersey for the Passover Seder celebration at Nana and Papa's home. On the way, we picked up Rachel from the Trenton train station, where she had arrived from New Haven. Jonny, Keiko and Tami (AJ's older brother and his family) were there, as was his younger brother Billy with his wife Beth and their sons Gaby, 10, and Alex, 7. Nana and Papa loved people and there were always various friends and neighbors present at their seders as well. When I saw Keiko, I showed off my new "nin" pendant.

"Ah, patience," she said smiling.

"That's what it takes," I replied, "patience and persistence."

It took some doing to get things settled down enough to begin the seder. Papa sat down, and we managed to gather everybody together. The Seder, meaning "order," is a traditional meal which includes telling the story of the Jews' enslavement in Egypt and deliverance to freedom led by Moses. It marks the beginning of the eight-day festival of Passover. In the center of the table is a Seder plate displaying symbolic foods. Matzoh, unleavened bread, is eaten as a reminder that the Jewish people departed from Egypt in such haste there was no time for bread to rise.

Among the blessings at the beginning of the Seder we recited the "Shehecheyanu" prayer:

"Praised are You Lord our God, Ruler of the universe, granting us life, sustaining us, and enabling us to reach this day."

References:

1. Malmstrom, C.D. "Bud". *Warriorship: Life Lessons of a Martial Artist.* Briarwood Publications, Inc., Rocky Mount Virginia, 2000, p.34.

15

On Hiatus

Sensei Bud Malmstrom, the Elrods' instructor, returned from Georgia the second weekend in May to conduct a seminar on gun defenses. We worked with wooden handguns, not the real thing, although the techniques were applicable to both.

"Draw the attacker close in and then quickly grab the gun, turning it against the weakest part of your opponent's grip. At the same time, move your entire body out of the line of the attack," he taught. In order to be effective, the defense must be rapid and decisive.

I thought it would be a good idea to consult a nutritionist during the month between chemotherapy and radiation. After all, Bonnie had a wonderful herbalist. Maybe it would help build up my system.

I made an appointment with the nutritionist at a local "wellness" clinic. After I completed a detailed questionnaire about my medical history, the nutritionist took me back to his office and reviewed my information. He said it was good that I had come after the completion of chemotherapy and before radiation because my liver should be cleansed of all the toxins. To accomplish that, he prescribed omega fatty acid tablets to increase the bile flow in my liver, as well as vitamins to eliminate any deficiency I might have developed. I was to take 12 of the vitamin tablets per day, four with each meal. I dutifully shelled out $60 for the purchases.

It wasn't until I got home that I looked carefully at the labels. Each individual vitamin was equivalent to one of AJ's multivitamins, and I was supposed to take 12 per day! That added up to 30,000 units of vitamin A. Vitamin A, an antioxidant, is one of the fat-soluble vitamins that can build up in the body and cause toxicity when taken in excessive amounts. Additionally, the vitamins contained no iron or calcium. I was still anemic, working on building up my hemoglobin, and I needed that iron. In my newly post-menopausal state, calcium supplementation was extremely important to prevent bone loss. The two minerals my body needed, and they weren't there.

I just happened to receive an issue of *Ca A Cancer Journal for Clinicians* that day. As luck would have it, that particular issue was devoted to nutrition for cancer patients. One of the articles mentioned that antioxidants should not be taken during radiation therapy, as they might interfere with the mechanism of action and effectiveness.[1]

If I hadn't had access to medical resources, I might not have known that I shouldn't take megadoses of vitamins. While Dr. Minford had warned me against taking any herbal products on chemotherapy, I had considered vitamins to be different. This underscores the importance of checking with an oncologist before adding any supplements to the mix.

I relayed the experience to Gordon when I saw him the following day. What do patients who aren't physicians do? We agreed that people really needed to be careful about what's out there.

I remarked how there is such controversy about screening mammography, with its proven benefits. Yet people go in droves to natural food stores and buy all sorts of herbs and supplements, not even regulated by the FDA. Who knows what's in them? They haven't been subjected to randomized controlled studies to prove their worth. Dr. Harmon Eyre in his editorial, "Nutritional Advice for Cancer Survivors," stated it succinctly:

"Despite the relative lack of evidence on many of these issues, there is no lack of opinions—many of which are offered with a degree of certainty that is out of proportion to the degree of evidence available."[2]

Acupuncture at least has 3000 years of experience behind it, not to mention clinical trials supporting its use.[3,4]

AJ and I met with Dr. Sally Cheston, the radiation oncologist, the second week in May. I'd met Sally before at meetings when we both served on the hospital's cancer committee. Her sunny, kind presence is a definite asset for someone in her chosen field.

After reviewing my chart, Sally examined me. She then proceeded to explain to us what the treatments would entail. First there would be a planning session, which would last about 45 minutes. Following that, there would be a total of 33 treatments: 25 to the entire breast and the axillary and supraclavicular lymph nodes, followed by 8 electron boost treatments to the surgical site.

Potential side effects include redness, as well as desquamation of the skin (i.e., skin peeling off), which sometimes necessitates a delay in completion of treatment. Radiation pneumonitis (inflammation of the lung) could also occur. Rarely, there are delayed adverse effects, such as a primary bone tumor in the area.

Having done much of my radiology residency training at a cancer hospital, I was familiar with these possible complications. But the substantial benefits of radiation therapy after lumpectomy far outweigh the risks. Namely, radiation after lumpectomy results in survival rates comparable to mastectomy and a marked decrease in the rate of breast cancer recurrence.[5] Amen.

At work later in the week I was sitting at the mammography viewbox reading screening studies when one of the technologists came in to show me a diagnostic case. It was an annual check-up on a woman four years out from lumpectomy, chemotherapy and radiation for breast cancer. I put the films up on the viewbox, along with mammograms from previous years for comparison.

I saw it immediately. The enemy had returned. In the treated breast, there was a new density about two inches away from the site of the original lumpectomy. At my request, the technologist performed additional spot compression views to confirm its presence. It didn't go away. I showed the patient her films with the new area of density and told her that the next step would be to do an ultrasound to see if the new lesion was a cyst or solid tissue.

"I don't think I can deal with this," she said, as she had other serious health problems. The ultrasound technologist worked her into the schedule a few minutes later. The patient was positioned on the ultrasound table when I walked into the room. Based on the mammogram, I knew where the lesion should be, and I placed the ultrasound probe in the area.

There it was: a small, hypoechoic, sound-absorbing mass with lobulated margins, ultrasound features suspicious for malignancy. I then told the patient that there was a new solid mass, which should be biopsied to determine what it was. Her next step would be to speak with her oncologist and surgeon. Since we could see it by ultrasound, we could do a needle biopsy under ultrasound guidance. The patient knew all too well about the procedure from her original diagnosis.

She took it all in. I contacted her oncologist whom she spoke to right away. I hugged her, and she somberly thanked me as she left my office.

How could it come back after all that surgery, chemotherapy, and radiation? And in someone who was plagued by other health problems, as well. It was so unfair. I'm learning that life isn't about fairness. It's about playing the hand you're dealt the best way possible.

The case haunted me the rest of the day. My job exposes me to all the "what-ifs." I can never take life for granted. Each day is a precious gift, a jewel, to be cherished while it's in our hands. Here and now, that's what we've got. I must make the most of every moment.

"The secret to happiness is happiness itself. Wherever we are, any time, we have the capacity to enjoy the sunshine, the presence of each other, the wonder of our breathing."[6]

Rachel finished her final exams and was home for Mother's Day. AJ prepared our favorite feast of standing rib roast with pan-roasted potatoes, the reason I could never become a vegetarian. For dessert we enjoyed my gifts of Godiva chocolates. The best Mother's Day gift of all was just being there, enjoying my husband and children.

References:

1. Brown J, Byers T, Thompson K, et al. Nutrition During and After Cancer Treatment: A Guide for Informed Choices by Cancer Survivors. Ca A Cancer Journal for Clinicians 2001;51:153-181.

2. Eyre, HJ. Nutritional Advice for Cancer Survivors. Ca A Cancer Journal for Clinicians 2001;51:151-152.

3. Shen J, Wenger N, Glaspy J, et al. Electroacupuncture for control of Myeloablative chemotherapy-induced emesis: A randomized controlled trial. JAMA 2000;284:2755-2761.

4. Cardini F, Weixin H. Moxibustion for correction of breech presentation: A randomized controlled trial. JAMA 1998;280:1580-1584.

5. Fisher B, Anderson S, Bryant J, et al. Twenty-year follow-up of a randomized trial comparing total mastectomy, lumpectomy, and lumpectomy plus irradiation for the treatment of invasive breast cancer. N Engl J Med 2002;347:1233-1241.

6. Hanh, Thich Nhat. *Peace is Every Step: The Path of Mindfulness in Everyday Life*. Bantam Books, New York, 1991, p.78.

16

Catching Some Rays

"Working with your partner, both of you close your eyes," instructed Mrs. Elrod. You'll each try to take your partner to the ground, off-balancing and using grabs. Since your eyes will be closed, go slowly. Feel where your partner is and how you can counter each grab. Feel the energy of each attack and use it for your defense." I used to train in a dojo with a blind martial artist—he was phenomenal. Concentrate, focus on balance and technique.

At acupuncture, I frequently asked questions about the different points. I loved to hear their names, not just the meridian and number, such as stomach 36, but the other names that reflected the history and spirit of the points: the aspirin point, to relieve joint and muscular aches; the leg three mile point, used by Chinese soldiers, who would rub this point on their shins to march another three miles when they were fatigued.

At ten o'clock on a bright May morning I arrived at the outpatient oncology center for my radiation simulation appointment. I met the technologist Janet who took me back to the simulation room. First, a mold was made of my upper body. I was positioned on the mold-casting material, which was a squishy substance. Janet placed my left arm above my head, in the position it would be for the radiation treatments. I had to lie still for several minutes as the mold set. The material became warm from the ensuing chemical reaction. It felt like lying on the warm sand of a beach. This wasn't bad at all!

Once the mold was created, several x-rays were taken at different angles. Sally showed them to me afterwards. They were quite different than those we use in Diagnostic Radiology. The focus was on soft tissues and tangential angles to my rib cage, rather than the rib or heart and lung detail I was accustomed to viewing. The soft tissue detail was not like that on mammogram images, either.

Sally pointed out the surgical clips that Dr. Schnaper had placed at the surgical site, which were very helpful for planning the treatment. The x-rays taken were used to calculate the precise angle of the radiation therapy beams, carefully avoiding unnecessary exposure to the underlying heart and lungs. I was all in favor of that!

I could see where someone not as familiar with radiology equipment as I am might find the machinery intimidating. I'm used to working with it, and regard it as friend, not foe. Once all of the angles were calculated, Janet carefully marked the ports on my skin using a blue Sharpie magic marker. No tattoos, fortunately. She said I needed to be careful not to wash the lines off, by turning so that the shower water wouldn't directly beat down on the area. Also, she advised me to wear bras I didn't mind getting stained with the blue ink.

I was prescribed a soothing cream, Biafine, to apply to the site at night if it became irritated. No creams over the area before the treatment. No aluminum-containing antiperspirants. I bought a "natural" deodorant, which Sally recommended. Every life experience is an opportunity to shop.

My treatment started the following week. I requested an early morning time slot, 7:15 a.m., so I could head off to work afterwards. It would become available the second week of my treatment. The scheduler at the front desk was very accommodating. Vicki had written the work schedule so that I was assigned to the office half a block away from the oncology center during my radiation therapy. I had also arranged to take two weeks off: the last week of my treatment and the week after that to rest.

Before I started my early morning treatment time, I would sit in the waiting room with others scheduled for treatments. I was frequently the youngest one there, just as I had been in the chemotherapy suite. Cancer recognizes no age restrictions.

Once I started my 7:15 a.m. therapy routine, I opened up the shop with the techs: I was the first patient on the schedule. With such complicated equipment, unanticipated breakdowns can occur. I was warned of that, although I knew it all too well from my own experience with fluoroscopy and CT scanning equipment. I'm grateful to say that the equipment behaved itself for my 33 treatments. There was only one morning when it didn't boot up correctly, and I had to return later in the day. As I was working right down the street, that posed no problem.

Radiation was quite relaxing. The technologists did everything they could to make the atmosphere as pleasant as possible. There was always music playing in the background. After the day they played country western, though, I decided to bring my own CD's to listen to during the treatments. I preferred piano jazz.

I was in and out of there in 20 minutes, with each treatment only lasting about 10 minutes. The technologists positioned me on my mold on the table.

Lining up the equipment to the marks on my skin, they applied the x-ray beams from different angles to cover the area.

I consciously used the time for relaxation and focused positive visualization. I wanted to do everything I could to help my body with the radiation. To minimize the skin reaction, I visualized the skin of my breast wrapped in a protective coating of Saran wrap. The salutary beams of radiation would penetrate deeper, going right to the tissue intended. I received radiation to the breast and the axillary and supraclavicular (right above the clavicle) lymph nodes. Interestingly, I initially visualized only the breast and underarm wrapped in the plastic wrap. When I developed a pink area over the supraclavicular site, I added it to my Saran wrap visualization and the skin then had no further reaction!

There was plenty of time to conjure up all sorts of positive imagery. First there was the cleansing imagery that I had used during chemotherapy. I imagined the radiation as a dryer, getting rid of any stray malignant cells in the surgical bed or lymph nodes. I then gravitated to poolside imagery, with the radiation as the warm, soothing sun. My cells were healthy cells, like big handsome lifeguards sitting around the pool (why not enjoy your imagery?).

June 1, 2001, my 47th birthday. I've always enjoyed my birthday, but this was one I was really glad to see. The past few years, I had taken it as a vacation day from work. This day began with a warm, sunny morning. After my treatment, I went home to walk Meg O'Bite and check e-mail, then was off to the gym. It was my day, to do what I wanted.

For dinner, AJ, Michael, and I went to a Japanese hibachi steakhouse. Rachel was back at school working at the alumni reunion weekend. She called just as we were having cake at home, as if she were there celebrating with us. Everyone called in: Mom, Wayne, Leslie, Debbie. After the past few months, my birthday had taken on new meaning. Truly a celebration, I will never bemoan getting older, but take it as a gift of another year to make the most of and to treasure.

In the first two weeks of June, my eyebrows completely grew back. They were the last hair to thin out and the first to grow back. I carefully monitored the thickening hair on my head. While my birthday came and went and I was still wearing Doris, I knew she wouldn't be with me for long. Great timing—wigs are rather warm for Maryland's hot, humid summers.

The morning radiation treatments became part of my routine. On my days off I liked to reward myself with a Starbucks afterwards. Since I had to be particularly careful in the sun after radiation, I used the opportunity to buy myself a sun hat at J.C. Penney in the mall. At the gym, my energy level was holding steady, a balance between the blood counts coming up and the radiation slowing me down. Taking it slow and steady, I kept up the amount and repetitions of the weights I was lifting.

On workdays I went to radiation and arrived at my office before eight. On my last day of work, after five weeks of radiation, I felt somewhat weary. I noticed muscle aches towards the end of the day. Once home, I took my temperature: I had a low-grade fever of about 99.5 and went right to bed. It was a good thing I had arranged some time off for a little r, r, and r (radiation, rest, and relaxation).

Rachel was home for only a couple of weeks before her summer in China. We shopped for the odds and ends she needed for her trip: clothing, travel accessories, just the right duffle to fit everything. At the same time, Michael was busy preparing for his summer program in Tanglewood.

June 20, 2001, nearly the beginning of summer: Rachel and Michael decided we should all go to the Baltimore Symphony Orchestra together, before they left for their separate adventures. Michael was particularly interested in hearing the young pianist Lang Lang who was a featured soloist. We all dressed up for the event. I wore my little black dress and the new gold earrings AJ had just given me for my birthday. But the big deal was my hair: Doris stayed home. It was the debut of the chic new me with short hair.

17

Back on the Road Again

At the end of a tiring class of sparring and spontaneous techniques, Mrs. Elrod sat us down around the edge of the training mat for a meditation exercise.

"Your brain can't tell the difference between what actually happens and your visualization," she said. "By imagining yourself successfully defending against an actual attack, you can help yourself train." The room was darkened, soft music started playing.

"Close your eyes," began Mrs. Elrod. "You're at the mall, arms full of heavy packages. It's cold, dark, you're walking to your car." The music grew louder and more intense. Mrs. Elrod then described a vivid encounter with the scariest foe we could imagine: the startling attack, fear, self-defense, fatigue, determination to go on, and ultimate success, driving in our car back to the safety of home. It was frightening, but we prevailed, made it, alive, safe, and unharmed.

I opened my eyes, still shaking, my heart pounding from the imagined altercation, but also filled with confidence of success, a win. I had met the enemy and prevailed.

Shi-kin hara-mitsu dai-ko-myo: "Every encounter could present the one potential key to...enlightenment."

Sen-sei ni rei: "Bow to salute the teacher."

Do-mo a-ri-ga-to go-zai-mas: "Thank you very much [for teaching me]."[1]

The last eight treatments consisted of a radiation boost to the surgical site. Those treatments went quickly. The actual treatment probably took less than two minutes, and I was in and out of the oncology center in about fifteen minutes.

June 28, 2001: Oh glorious, long awaited day—my last radiation treatment! This time, AJ drove me. We arrived in the quiet, somber waiting room all smiles, carrying a bouquet of balloons in appreciation of the wonderful staff. In and out of the treatment room within five minutes.

My radiation was over. I jumped off the table and out of the room. The technologist Janet asked if I wanted to keep the mold used for me, some patients did as a souvenir. No thank you, my healthy breast was all the souvenir I needed.

I thought of the prayer said upon recovery from such things as surgery or trauma, so appropriate for me at that moment:

"Praised are You Lord our God, who rules the universe, showing goodness to us beyond our merits, for bestowing favor upon me," followed by the Congregation's response:

"May God who has been gracious to you continue to favor you with all that is good."[2]

AJ and I celebrated by going to a Tex-Mex restaurant near the mall for lunch. This was one chapter of our lives we were glad to have behind us.

I had read about and was prepared for the possibility of a let down or depression following completion of therapy. With the support of psychotherapy and acupuncture, however, I thought it unlikely. Besides, I started Tamoxifen two weeks after finishing radiation, so at least I was still doing something to prevent It from returning. In five years, after completion of the course of Tamoxifen, how would I feel? Let's get to the five-year point and celebrate that moment when it comes.

Tamoxifen, which acts like a weak estrogen, blocks estrogen receptors in breast tissue, although it has an estrogen-like effect on the lining of the uterus. The latter causes a small increased risk of endometrial cancer. Other estrogenic effects result in risks of deep vein thrombosis (blood clots) and pulmonary embolism (clots to the lungs). Its antiestrogenic effect on breast tissue, though, results in an almost 50% reduction in breast cancer recurrence or second breast cancer.

It's good to know there's something out there to reduce risk, since we don't know what exactly causes breast cancer. Chemoprevention: an idea whose time has come. I welcomed the Tamoxifen. It marked the end of chemotherapy and radiation and the beginning of prevention. Each night, as I take the small white pill, I raise my water glass in a toast and sing "L'Chayim," to life!

Note: since the time of my treatment, new clinical studies have shown advantages of treatment by aromatase inhibitors, following or in place of Tamoxifen, for post-menopausal women with estrogen receptor positive early breast cancers.[3,4] Aromatase inhibitors prevent estrogen production by the body and are associated with fewer side effects as well as lower incidences of breast cancer recurrences and second primaries. Dr. Minford switched me to the aromatase inhibitor Arimidex 6 months after I started the Tamoxifen. Duration of treatment with aromatase inhibitors is still being investigated.

My hair had grown back in a duller color, with more gray than I would have liked. In the first week of July I made an appointment with my hairdresser Lisa for a color and trim. It was my first appointment with her since November. I was so excited to have hair and get it actually colored and styled that I was practically bouncing in her chair. Lisa still had the recipe for my hair tint that she'd used for the past several years. She applied the youth and wellness in a bottle. An hour later, I looked ten years younger, with a short, stylish haircut.

With chemotherapy complete, my counts back up, and radiation finished, I was ready to do some traveling. The first trip was to see my mother in Florida. It was an easy flight from Baltimore-Washington airport to Fort Lauderdale. My mother had arranged for a driver to pick me up, a pleasant woman about my age, who had started out driving her own mother's acquaintances and now earned a living doing it.

Mom! It was so great to see her. She beamed at me with love and relief to see me looking well, having survived the ordeal of the past eight months. The hair was a little short, maybe I should brush back the bangs a little, make it look more feminine.

My mother lives a quiet, contemplative life. Being with her provided respite, a period of recovery for me. We exchanged books. I gave her *Anatomy of the Spirit* by Carolyn Myss, and she introduced me to the writing of Louise Hays. I swam in the neighborhood pool. We went out to dinner, took evening walks through the community, and just spent time being together.

When I returned home I noticed trouble sleeping, waking at frequent intervals during the night with difficulty getting back to sleep. Sandy treated "Anmian," the sleep point behind the ears. I felt a sense of peacefulness during the session. Although I came in with physical symptoms to be treated, Sandy treated the bodymindspirit as one. I emerged from the acupuncture session feeling that my spirit had been touched, shifted into another, more serene, place.

Michael was enjoying his summer at Tanglewood, studying French horn, as well as playing piano with a couple of chamber music groups. Rachel called us from China to let us know all was well. Her program required a language pledge: the students were only allowed to speak Chinese, except, of course, when calling those of us at home who didn't speak the language. During portions of our telephone conversation, Rachel lapsed into Chinese. When I said "What?" she laughed and switched back into English.

She mentioned that one of her friends' mothers was coming to visit. Would I be able to come to travel with her at the end of the program, the last week in August? I was thrilled. I told her I would check my work schedule to make sure I could arrange it and would e-mail her back as soon as I knew. Within a day, I had cleared it with our physician scheduler Vicki and booked myself a roundtrip ticket to Beijing.

The last week in July, AJ and I joined three of my high school friends and their husbands at the house in Martha's Vineyard that we rented together. Debbie, Peter and Rebecca were there, along with Rebecca's friend Olivia. Rene and her husband Andy, and Jackie and her husband Scott. We rode bikes, played tennis, cooked sumptuous dinners, went to the beach, and simply relaxed. I taught Rebecca and Olivia karate techniques: rolls, punches and kicks, tips on rescuing a friend. At the end of the week, we had a karate demo, to a background of lively music they had selected.

Debbie, Jackie, Rene and I spent the rainy day during the week shopping. Jackie introduced us to her favorite Martha's Vineyard clothing store. We lingered in a shop of handcrafted jewelry while picking out earrings to go with my new short 'do. When we returned to the house, we made a delicious layered Mexican bean dip together, chopping vegetables and chatting. The husbands and children were off on their own adventures. We enjoyed frozen daiquiris with the chips and dip, sitting around the kitchen table laughing and telling stories, our Yankee Ya-Ya Sisterhood.

A month later, I was off to Beijing. My flight connected from Baltimore-Washington International to O'Hare airport in Chicago, with a change of planes to Beijing. Due to thunderstorms around O'Hare, my Baltimore flight was delayed in taking off. As a result, I missed my connecting flight to Beijing. I was then booked on a flight with a change of planes in Tokyo. I had no way of telling Rachel about the revised plans, but I called AJ, hoping that she'd call him when I didn't show up as scheduled. Rachel had just returned from traveling in southern China, hadn't slept the night before, watched the sun rise and flag-raising ceremony at Tiananmen square, and proceeded to spend the entire day waiting for me at the airport. When I deplaned, I went through customs, gazing at the vast airport and huge number of people in it. Among them was Rachel! Glory be, she'd gotten the updated itinerary by telephoning AJ. I was mighty relieved to see her.

After two months in China, Rachel felt quite comfortable there. She loved the summer program she was in and had learned a tremendous amount, typically forty Chinese characters a night. That was like learning an entire alphabet daily! During weekends and the midterm break she had traveled around different parts of China with other students in the program.

As we got into a cab, I was amazed to hear Rachel converse in Chinese with the driver, giving him directions to our hotel. It was dark and hard to see much during the ride. Rachel had booked a room at a hotel with the gym she'd used during the summer, so the personnel knew her. When we arrived, she introduced me to her acquaintance Sam the bellboy who helped us with our luggage. At first he didn't believe that I was Rachel's mother since he thought I looked too young. That certainly was nice to hear after surgery, chemotherapy, radiation, and twenty-four hours of traveling.

Having spent the summer in Beijing, Rachel was familiar with many of its highlights. Our first day, we visited the college campus where she'd lived, as well as the surrounding neighborhood and shops. We toured the nearby estate of Madame Song, wife of Sun Yat-Sen where I encountered my first view of history from the other side of the world, with reference to the liberation of China in 1949. Rachel took my picture by the early 20th century x-ray machine in the museum. When we walked outside, we saw a bride and groom being photographed on the beautifully kept grounds.

Rachel easily navigated us around on the extensive subway system. Not speaking any Chinese, I was entirely dependent on my daughter in this new environment. I had first hand empathy for immigrants to the U.S. who don't speak English and rely on their children to negotiate daily life. On the other hand, having no English speakers around liberated us to say exactly what we pleased. Walking through the tunnels of the subway system, Rachel would look at a stocky Chinese man and turn to me and say:

"His name is Ralph."

I began to pick up a few Chinese words here and there, what I call "Rachel" Chinese, because I heard her use these phrases. For example, "zhei ge," means "this," which Rachel would say when she pointed to something on a menu or in a shop; "wo-men," means "us," and, of course, I understood "Ma," when she was talking about me. We decided there wouldn't be quite enough time to have a "Qi-pao" (formal Chinese dress) custom made for me.

We took a subway ride to a beautiful Buddhist temple in Beijing, where there were a series of buildings housing progressively larger Buddha statues, until we got to the largest one "Yi da Buddha" (one big Buddha), which was several stories tall.

Three days later we took an overnight train to Xian to see the terracotta soldiers. We shared our compartment with an ophthalmologist and his wife, who were commuting to work. Through Rachel as our interpreter, we chatted about medical practice in China and the U.S. He was under the impression that my salary was much larger than it actually was.

We arrived in Xian late in the morning. The area around the train station was crowded with people pushing towards us trying to sell us souvenirs or taxi rides.

"Bu yao," (I don't want any) we said as we made our way through the crowd.

"No," I said, shaking my head. Then I went back to "Bu yao."

We selected a taxi and made our way to the hotel. Once settled, we arranged for a tour of the terracotta soldiers for the following day and then explored the city of Xian. It was a steaming hot August day. We each carried a bottle of water and enjoyed fruit ices from a stand. For lunch, we ate at a restaurant famous for its "jiaozi," dumplings in all sorts of flavors and shapes, such as flowers and dragons.

The next day, we took an English-language tour of the terracotta soldiers. I was relieved to be able to understand a language again. The soldiers are a life-sized army of several thousand on foot and horseback. The details were so realistic, with every feature clearly sculpted. What a tribute to the emperor they honored! We also visited the summer palace of the emperor, as well as the Muslim quarter, which contained a serene temple, a quiet respite from the surrounding bustling city.

We took a plane back to Beijing for the last two days of the trip. There, we visited the Forbidden City and Tiananmen Square, with the large picture of Mao Tse Tung overlooking it. We even had frappuccinos at the nearby Starbucks!

Rachel had saved the best for our last day: the Great Wall of China. After a short subway ride, we arrived at the bus station, where we caught a somewhat rickety bus for the two-hour ride to the Great Wall. The roads in the last part of the trip were unpaved, which made for a bumpy ride. About an hour and a half outside of Beijing, my eyes started stinging terribly due to some particulate pollutant in the air. I could barely keep them open. Fortunately, by the time we arrived at our destination the wind had shifted and my eyes were fine.

Rachel had done this particular four-hour hike of the Great Wall earlier in the summer with a group of her friends. It was a difficult hike and, consequently, less crowded and touristy than some of the others. I was apprehensive.

"Ma, you can do it. You've been going to the gym," reassured Rachel. We started our trek along the rocks that comprised the Great Wall. It wasn't too bad in the beginning.

"Mei wenti," Chinese for "No problem," Rachel taught me. After about forty-five minutes we encountered a steep vertical ascent. Having no experience in rock climbing, I did not know how to negotiate it.

"I'll go up first so I can help you," said Rachel. She climbed up the sloping rocks to the plateau. I watched as she grabbed on with her hands and hoisted herself up on the rocks. Then I tried to do the same, but I didn't have the arm strength to carry myself up.

"Rache," I said, "I don't think I can do it." I struggled a few minutes, with her trying to help me up. Out of nowhere, an elderly Chinese man appeared. He gave me his hand and boosted me up to the plateau. Almost as quickly as he appeared, he disappeared. An angel of the Great Wall!

The strenuous climb continued, up and down steep slopes.

"Ma, are you doing okay?" Rachel called back to me periodically.

"Mei wenti," I called back, as I plodded slowly behind her. I perfected "butt climbing," sitting down on the rocks and sliding slowly down for the descent. Each step required intense concentration to find the steadiest rocks for balance. I could think of nothing else, for if my thoughts wandered but a moment I would find myself slipping. The required deep concentration rivaled anything I'd experienced in my medical career. Rachel and I each had episodes of slipping several feet. We promised each other we wouldn't die up here in these remote mountains, half a world away from the rest of our family.

Three hours later the trail ended with a steep descent, which required stepping down on the rocks, using them as a ladder. Rachel led the way, falling a couple of feet. I yelled to her to see if she was all right.

"Fine, but my watchstrap broke," she called back. Then it was my turn. I didn't know which rocks to step on. Hesitantly, I tried one and then another, but they each slipped under my weight. Miraculously, another "angel of the Wall," this time, a woman, appeared. Knowing no English, she pointed to each rock for me to place my feet. With her assistance, I made it to the bottom of the trail.

My legs were shaking with fatigue. It was good to sit down in the chairs the woman provided outside her small hut. Rachel chatted with her in Chinese, and we bought sodas. They were the best Sprites in the world, partially frozen, ice cold and refreshing. We savored the taste of survival and accomplishment.

References:

1. Hayes, SK. *Enlightened Self-Protection: The Kasumi-An Ninja Arts Tradition.* Nine Gates Press, 1992, p.21.

2. The Rabbinical Assembly: the United Synagogue of Conservative Judaism. *Siddur Sim Shalom for Shabbat and Festivals.* The Rabbinical Assembly, 1998.

3. Buzda AU. Data from the Arimidex, tamoxifen, alone or in combination (ATAC) trial: implications for use of aromatase inhibitors in 2003. Clin Cancer Res 2004;10:355S-361S.

4. Coombes RC, Hall E, Gibson L, et al. A randomized trial of exemestane after two to three years of tamoxifen therapy in postmenopausal women with primary breast cancer. N Eng J Med 2004;350:1081-1092.

Epilogue

◆

Third Degree Black Belt Test: March 1, 2003

Mr. and Mrs. Elrod came to me last September and said:
"We'd like you to test for your third degree black belt next winter." I thought to myself: "Third degree?! I'm nowhere near ready. But, Mr. and Mrs. Elrod are excellent, experienced teachers, and if they think I'll be ready, I'm going to work hard and do it." So here I am. I made it!

Training at the white belt level, learning all those new kicks and punches, was so easy. I wondered when it was going to get hard. Then, two to three years later at red belt, struggling to learn the dive rolls and sparring, I thought:

"This is so hard. When does it get easy? When will it seem as effortless as it looks for Mrs. Elrod? When will I be able to turn those multiple attackers into pretzels like Bud Malmstrom and Hatsumi Sensei do, without even breaking a sweat?"

The answer is: not yet. In training to go from second to third degree black belt, I've worked as hard as I have for anything in my entire life. I was up against a foe tougher than the guy who threw me when I was a red belt, resulting in my shoulder separation; tougher than the multiple six-foot 200+ lb. attackers they threw at me going to second degree. My adversary: breast cancer, and I was fighting for life itself.

Over two years ago, I sat down with Mrs. Elrod to tell her about my recent diagnosis. I told her I wanted to keep training as much as I could.

"You'll do fine," she said, "you're a fighter." Those words stuck with me during surgery, chemotherapy, and radiation. And, I kept training through it all. I had to go easy on the sparring for a few months, but I kept doing as much as I could safely do.

"All I need is hemoglobin, and I wouldn't be so out of breath," I thought as I tired more easily on the bagwork. During one class, my cap fell off while I was rolling, revealing my bald head. I put it right back on and kept rolling. In the words of the Grandmaster Hatsumi Sensei:

"Keep going."

My training helped me face the treatments as well. Myalgias from Taxol chemotherapy were nothing compared to the sore muscles following a tough class of sparring. When my counts were down and I was fatigued, I rested but had faith and kept going, saying to myself:

"The spirit is strong, though the body is weak; I'm going to get through this."

So here I am. I've kept going, kept training, and it's paid off. More than two years later, I'm disease-free, standing here in fighting form. My being here is a tribute to Mr. and Mrs. Elrod, with their fine teaching, encouragement, and faith in me through it all. I must also thank my doctors and modern medicine, my friends and family for their loving support, particularly my husband AJ who has been there through it all (although after first degree black belt, we couldn't practice on him anymore) and my children Rachel and Michael, who have trained side by side with me these twelve plus years.

And, I stand on the shoulders of giants. I close by honoring the memories of two warriors who fell before me: Mrs. Elrod's mother Julie Smith who set an example of valiantly fighting this battle, and my father-in-law Robert Alpert, a World War II veteran who persevered to the end, defying all odds.

Note: Papa Bob Alpert passed away June 23, 2002.

Glossary

Acupuncture: ancient Chinese medical science based on the flow of energy (**Qi**) in the body. Treatments consist of the placement of tiny, threadlike needles along the body's "meridians," energy pathways.

Anemia: low **red blood cell (rbc)** count, also measured by **hematocrit** (percent of red blood cells in the blood by volume). As rbc's are responsible for carrying oxygen in the blood (in the form of **hemoglobin**), a decrease in their number can result in fatigue and reduced exercise tolerance.

Anesthesia: administration of medication to reduce or alleviate pain. **Local anesthesia** refers to applying a numbing substance directly to an area; in **general anesthesia**, the patient is asleep during an operation, with assisted breathing (intubation). In **twilight sleep** or **conscious sedation,** the patient is not totally unconscious, but will not be aware of pain or remember the procedure.

Aromatase inhibitors: drugs which block estrogen production by the body. They are used after or in place of **tamoxifen** to inhibit tumor cell growth in postmenopausal women with estrogen sensitive tumors.

Biopsy: removal of tissue for analysis by a pathologist. **Excisional biopsy** (lumpectomy) refers to removal of an abnormal growth in its entirety. **Incisional biopsy** (core biopsy) entails removing tissue samples from a lesion, not the whole thing.

Bone marrow: central cavity of bone. In the larger bones, the marrow is the site of blood cell production, including red blood cells, white blood cells, and platelets.

Bujinkan Ninpo Taijutsu: 900-year-old Japanese martial art, practitioners of which are commonly known as Ninjas.

Chemotherapy: the treatment of cancer by cell-killing (cytoxic) medications.

CT scan or CAT scan: Computed Assisted Tomography, a computerized x-ray examination that images thin cross-sectional slices through the body. It can be performed on a variety of structures, from head to feet.

Cyst: fluid-filled sac. Cysts can occur in the breast as well as in other parts of the body, such as the ovary.

DCIS (ductal cancer in situ): localized breast cancer that originates from cells lining the ducts and remains limited to the ducts, not involving surrounding breast tissue.

Dose dense chemotherapy: chemotherapy administered at two-week rather than the traditional three-week intervals.

Ducts: tubular structures. In the breast, the milk (lactiferous) ducts connect the milk-producing lobules to the nipple. At least 8-15 ducts drain into each nipple.

Gi: karate uniform, consisting of a jacket, pants and belt (**obi**).

HER-2 *neu*: human epidermal growth factor receptor which, when overexpressed (present to a greater extent than on normal cells), indicates a more aggressive tumor. Such tumors are responsive to treatment with Herceptin, an antibody against the HER-2 *neu* protein.

Hormone therapy: treatment of cancer by changing the hormone levels in the body. In breast cancer sensitive to estrogen, **tamoxifen** and/or **aromatase inhibitors** are given to alter the hormonal environment and inhibit tumor cell growth.

Immunohistochemical staining: laboratory technique using immune responses (antibodies) to identify individual cells.

Infiltrating ductal carcinoma (invasive ductal cancer): cancer originating from the milk ducts, which has spread within the breast to the surrounding tissue.

Infiltrating lobular carcinoma (invasive lobular cancer): cancer originating from the breast lobules, which has spread within the breast to surrounding tissue.

IV (intravenous catheter): small tube used to administer fluid or medicine directly into the vein.

Leukopenia: low **white blood cell (wbc)** count. White blood cells are involved in the body's immune responses. A decrease in their number results in greater risk of infection.

Lobules: the milk-producing structures of the breast.

Lumpectomy: surgical removal of a tumor and rim of surrounding tissue.

Lymph nodes: glands located in many different parts of the body. Their function is to fight cells foreign to the body such as infections. They are also potential sites for the spread of cancer. Breast cancer most frequently involves the **axillary** (underarm) and to a lesser extent the **supraclavicular** (above the collar bone) lymph nodes.

Magnification/spot compression views: mammogram images obtained using magnification and localized compression to visualize greater detail of breast tissue.

Mammogram: x-ray examination of the breasts. **Screening mammograms** are performed for the detection of disease in asymptomatic women. **Diagnostic mammograms** are obtained to evaluate breast problems. To optimally image all of the breast tissue in 3 dimensions, views are obtained in two planes: **MLO (medio-lateral oblique)**, an oblique side to side view and **CC (cranio-caudad)**, an up and down projection. Additional views, such as a **90° medio-lateral** view (straight side to side view) may be obtained to help locate an abnormality.

Mastectomy: removal of the entire breast.

Metastasis: spread of cancer outside the organ of origin.

Microcalcifications: minute calcium deposits. In the breast they can occur in benign or malignant disease. Size, shape, density, and distribution (scattered or clustered) determine whether they appear benign, indeterminate, or malignant on a mammogram.

MRI = Magnetic Resonance Imaging: a modality using strong magnetic fields and changing radiofrequencies to create images of the internal structures of the body. MRI is used to identify the extent of breast cancer in certain clinical situations. Preliminary studies have shown it to be a valuable supplement to screening mammography in high risk women (e.g., women with a strong family history of breast cancer or one of the breast cancer genes).[1,2] MRI is also performed in women with complications from breast implants.

Myalgias: muscle aches.

Neupogen/filgrastim (white blood cell Colony Stimulating Factor): a drug used to enhance white blood cell production by the bone marrow.

Neuropathy: nerve dysfunction. When it involves the peripheral nerves (nerves outside of the brain and spinal cord), a pins and needles or numb sensation can result, particularly in the hands and feet.

Neutropenia: low number of **neutrophils,** a type of white blood cell instrumental in fighting infection.

"Nin" 忍: Japanese symbol signifying patience, perseverance, persistence.

Port, port-a-cath, or indwelling central venous catheter: intravenous device surgically placed under the skin in the chest. It is connected to a vein, which empties directly into the heart. Ports are used when veins in the arms (peripheral veins) are too small for the administration of chemotherapy.

Preoperative needle (or wire) localization: performed to find a lesion seen by imaging examination of the breast but which cannot be felt. A small wire is placed in the breast using mammographic, ultrasound, or MR guidance. The patient then proceeds to the operating room, where the surgeon removes the tissue surrounding the tip of the wire.

Procrit or Epogen = epoetin alfa (red blood cell Colony Stimulating Factor): a drug used to enhance red cell production by the bone marrow.

Proliferative index or rate: pathology measurement of tumor reproduction. A low proliferative index indicates a slower cell growth rate and a better prognosis than a cancer with a high proliferative index. Activity is commonly measured by one of two cellular markers: MIB-1 or KI-67.

Radiation therapy (radiotherapy): the treatment of cancer by using high-energy beams from x-rays and other sources.

Receptors: structures on the surface of cells. Biochemicals in the body attach to receptors to affect cellular function. The presence or absence of receptors for the hormones **estrogen** (ER) and **progesterone** (PR) carry prognostic significance in breast cancer.

Sentinel lymph nodes: the first or closest lymph nodes that a tumor is likely to spread to. In breast cancer these are located in the armpit.

Shingles: skin lesions caused by the chickenpox virus, which has remained dormant and erupts in a nerve distribution under stress or suppression of the immune system.

Specimen radiograph: x-ray of the breast tissue that has been surgically removed.

Stage: description of cancer by its size, involvement of nearby lymph nodes, and spread to other parts of the body (metastasis). For more details about individual stages, see Dr. Susan Love's Breast Book, page 338.[3]

Stereotactic core biopsy: a type of **incisional biopsy** (see biopsy) using mammography guidance. Mammogram images are obtained from two different angles. This enables the computerized equipment to accurately localize the abnormality for needle placement and tissue sampling.

Tamoxifen: a drug used in hormone therapy for breast cancer. It blocks estrogen receptors in breast tissue and hormone sensitive tumors, resulting in decreased risk of breast cancer recurrence or second breast cancer.

Taxanes: chemotherapy drugs originally derived from the bark and needles of the Pacific yew tree. These include **Taxol** (paclitaxel) and **Taxotere** (docetaxel).

Thrombocytopenia: low **platelet** count. Platelets are involved in the clotting function of the blood.

Ultrasound: diagnostic imaging study based on the use of sound waves reflected off tissues in the body.

References:

1. Kriege M, Brekelmans CTM, Boetes C, et al. Efficacy of MRI and Mammography for Breast-Cancer Screening in Women with a Familial or Genetic Predisposition. N Engl J Med 2004;351:427-437.

2. Warner E, Plewes DB, Hill KA, et al. Surveillance of *BRCA1* and *BRCA2* Mutation Carriers With Magnetic Resonance Imaging, Ultrasound, Mammography, and Clinical Breast Examination. JAMA 2004;292:1317-1325.

3. Love, SM. *Dr. Susan Love's Breast Book.* Perseus Publishing, 2000, p.338.

References

Introduction:

1. Jemal A, Tiwari RC, Murray T, et al. Cancer Statistics, 2004. CA Cancer J Clin 2004;54:8-29.

2. Seaward BL. Humor's healing potential. Health Prog 1992;73:66-70.

3. Erdman L. Laughter therapy for patients with cancer. Oncol Nurs Forum 1991;18:1359-1363.

Chapter I:

1. Hayes, SK. *Enlightened Self-Protection: The Kasumi-An Ninja Arts Tradition.* Nine Gates Press, 1992, p.21.

2. Shockney, L. *Breast Cancer Survivors' Club: A Nurse's Experience.* Real Health Books, 1999, p.8.

3. Fisher B, Bauer M, Margolese R, et al. Five-year results of a randomized clinical trial comparing total mastectomy and segmental mastectomy with or without radiation in the treatment of breast cancer. N Engl J Med 1985; 312:665-73.

4. Veronesi U, Cascinelli N, Mariani L, et al. Twenty-year follow-up of a randomized study comparing breast-conserving surgery with radical mastectomy for early breast cancer. N Engl J Med 2002;347:1227-1232.

Chapter III:

1. Hayes, SK. *Enlightened Self-Protection: The Kasumi-An Ninja Arts Tradition.* Nine Gates Press, 1992, p.22.

Chapter V:

1. Tabar L, Yen MF, Vitak B, et al. Mammography service screening and mortality in breast cancer patients: 20-year follow-up before and after introduction of screening. Lancet 2003;361:1405-1410.

2. Smith RA, Saslow D, Sawyer KA, et al. American Cancer Society Guidelines For breast cancer screening: update 2003. CA Cancer J Clin 2003;53:141-169.

3. Love, SM. *Dr. Susan Love's Breast Book.* Perseus Publishing, 2000.

4. Siegel, BS. *Love, Medicine and Miracles: Lessons Learned About Self Healing from a Surgeon's Experience with Exceptional Patients.* Harper Perennial 1998.

5. Siegel, BS. *Getting Ready: Preparing for Surgery Chemotherapy, and Other Treatments (Audiocassette).* Hay House Audio 1999.

Chapter VI:

1. Hatsumi, Masaaki. *Ninpo: Wisdom for Life.* Kihon Press, 2002, p.93-94.

2. Kuligowska E. Marie Sklodowska Curie: Inspirational Role Model and Mother of Science 1867-1934. Journal of Women's Imaging 2003;5:68-73.

Chapter VIII:

1. Connelly, Diane M. *Traditional Acupuncture: The Law of the Five Elements.* Traditional Acupuncture Institute, Columbia, MD, 1994, p.11.

Chapter IX:

1. Hatsumi, Masaaki. *Ninpo: Wisdom for Life.* Kihon Press, 2002, p.169.

Chapter X:

1. Mole, Peter. *Acupuncture: Energy Balancing for Body, Mind, & Spirit.* Element Books, Inc. Boston, MA 1992, p.27.

Chapter XI:

1. The Rabbinical Assembly: the United Synagogue of Conservative Judaism. *Siddur Sim Shalom for Shabbat and Festivals.* The Rabbinical Assembly, 1998, p.144.

Chapter XII:

1. Love, SM. *Dr. Susan Love's Breast Book.* Perseus Publishing, 2000, p.383.

2. Anselmo, Diane. *Women's Choices, Women's Lives: Learn from 30 Not So Ordinary Women How the Power of Choice Can Change Your Life.* IUniverse, Inc. Lincoln, NE 2002, p.87.

Chapter XIV:

1. Malmstrom, C.D. "Bud". *Warriorship: Life Lessons of a Martial Artist.* Briarwood Publications, Inc., Rocky Mount Virginia, 2000, p.34.

Chapter XV:

1. Brown J, Byers T, Thompson K, et al. Nutrition During and After Cancer Treatment: A Guide for Informed Choices by Cancer Survivors. Ca A Cancer Journal for Clinicians 2001;51:153-181.

2. Eyre, HJ. Nutritional Advice for Cancer Survivors. Ca A Cancer Journal for Clinicians 2001;51:151-152.

3. Shen J, Wenger N, Glaspy J, et al. Electroacupuncture for control of Myeloablative chemotherapy-induced emesis: A randomized controlled trial. JAMA 2000;284:2755-2761.

4. Cardini F, Weixin H. Moxibustion for correction of breech presentation: A randomized controlled trial. JAMA 1998;280:1580-1584.

5. Fisher B, Anderson S, Bryant J, et al. Twenty-year follow-up of a randomized trial comparing total mastectomy, lumpectomy, and lumpectomy plus irradiation for the treatment of invasive breast cancer. N Engl J Med 2002;347:1233-1241.

6. Hanh, Thich Nhat. *Peace is Every Step: The Path of Mindfulness in Everyday Life.* Bantam Books, New York, 1991, p.78.

Chapter XVII:

1. Hayes, SK. *Enlightened Self-Protection: The Kasumi-An Ninja Arts Tradition.* Nine Gates Press, 1992, p.21.

2. The Rabbinical Assembly: the United Synagogue of Conservative Judaism. *Siddur Sim Shalom for Shabbat and Festivals.* The Rabbinical Assembly, 1998.

3. Buzda AU. Data from the Arimidex, tamoxifen, alone or in combination (ATAC) trial: implications for use of aromatase inhibitors in 2003. Clin Cancer Res 2004;10:355S-361S.

4. Coombes RC, Hall E, Gibson L, et al. A randomized trial of exemestane after two to three years of tamoxifen therapy in postmenopausal women with primary breast cancer. N Eng J Med 2004;350:1081-1092.

Glossary:

1. Kriege M, Brekelmans CTM, Boetes C, et al. Efficacy of MRI and Mammography for Breast-Cancer Screening in Women with a Familial or Genetic Predisposition. N Engl J Med 2004;351:427-437.

2. Warner E, Plewes DB, Hill KA, et al. Surveillance of *BRCA1* and *BRCA2* Mutation Carriers With Magnetic Resonance Imaging, Ultrasound, Mammography, and Clinical Breast Examination. JAMA 2004;292:1317-1325.

3. Love, SM. *Dr. Susan Love's Breast Book.* Perseus Publishing, 2000, p.338.

0-595-33603-5

CPSIA information can be obtained at www.ICGtesting.com
Printed in the USA
BVOW08s0221220116

433881BV00001B/50/P